PRENTICE-HALL FOUNDATIONS OF PHILOSOPHY SERIES

Virgil Aldrich	PHILOSOPHY OF ART
William Alston	PHILOSOPHY OF LANGUAGE
Stephen Barker	PHILOSOPHY OF MATHEMATICS
Roderick Chisholm	THEORY OF KNOWLEDGE
William Dray	PHILOSOPHY OF HISTORY
William Frankena	ETHICS
Carl Hempel	PHILOSOPHY OF NATURAL SCIENCE
John Hick	PHILOSOPHY OF RELIGION
Sidney Hook	POLITICAL PHILOSOPHY
John Lenz	PHILOSOPHY OF EDUCATION
Richard Rudner	PHILOSOPHY OF SOCIAL SCIENCE
Wesley Salmon	LOGIC
Richard Taylor	METAPHYSICS

Elizabeth and Monroe Beardsley, editors

Metaphysics

METAPHYSICS

FOUNDATIONS OF PHILOSOPHY SERIES

Richard Taylor

Brown University

PRENTICE-HALL, INC. ENGLEWOOD CLIFFS, N.J.

M E T A P H Y S I C S , Taylor

FOUNDATIONS OF PHILOSOPHY SERIES

C 57850

Current printing (last digit):
13   12   11   10   9   8   7   6   5   4

PRENTICE-HALL INTERNATIONAL, INC., LONDON
PRENTICE-HALL OF AUSTRALIA, PTY., LTD., SYDNEY
PRENTICE-HALL OF CANADA, LTD., TORONTO
PRENTICE-HALL OF INDIA (PRIVATE) LTD., NEW DELHI
PRENTICE-HALL OF JAPAN, INC., TOKYO
PRENTICE-HALL DE MEXICO, S.A., MEXICO CITY

To Everett Nelson

amico vero

FOUNDATIONS

OF PHILOSOPHY

Many of the problems of philosophy are of such broad relevance to human concerns, and so complex in their ramifications, that they are, in one form or another, perennially present. Though in the course of time they yield in part to philosophical inquiry, they may need to be rethought by each age in the light of its broader scientific knowledge and deepened ethical and religious experience. Better solutions are found by more refined and rigorous methods. Thus, one who approaches the study of philosophy in the hope of understanding the best of what it affords will look for both fundamental issues and contemporary achievements.

Written by a group of distinguished philosophers, the Foundations of Philosophy Series aims to exhibit some of the main problems in the various fields of philosophy as they stand at the present stage of philosophical history.

While certain fields are likely to be represented in most introductory courses in philosophy, college classes differ widely in emphasis, in method of instruction, and in rate of progress. Every instructor needs freedom to change his course as his own philosophical interests, the size and makeup of his classes, and the needs of his students vary from year to year. The thirteen volumes in the Foundations of Philosophy Series—each complete in itself, but complementing the others—offer a new flexibility to the instructor, who can create his own textbook by combining several volumes as he wishes, and can choose different combinations at different times. Those volumes that are not used in an introductory course will be found valuable, along with other texts or collections of readings, for the more specialized upper-level courses.

ELIZABETH BEARDSLEY   MONROE BEARDSLEY

PREFACE

This little book constitutes an introduction to the problems of metaphysics, and not a system thereof. The problems discussed are those that seem basic to metaphysics. I have made no attempt to set forth a survey of the subject. A conscientious attempt has been made to discuss problems in the light of data or common-sense beliefs which all men, rightly or wrongly, are apt to hold, quite apart from any philosophical theories. The conclusions reached are sometimes tentative and often modified in subsequent parts of the discussion.

The first three chapters, all dealing with various aspects of the mind-body problem, are largely inconclusive, because the answers to the questions raised there are not, in my opinion, known by anyone. The seventh chapter sets forth two lines of thought which seem to me to be strong reasons for believing in the existence of a "creator of heaven and earth." Since such arguments always stir deep suspicions, it must be stressed that they were composed with no polemical motive. I have no interest whatever in persuading anyone either that God does, or does not, exist. The arguments are developed because they seem to have philosophical merit, whatever anyone might think of their conclusion.

Since references have been carefully avoided, the following acknowledgements are in order. There is, first of all, scarcely a page that does not reflect the inspiration I have received from my colleague and former teacher Roderick Chisholm, though I have probably said rather little with which he would agree. The approach in Chapter 1 was, as will be obvious, suggested by Descartes' *Meditations*. The cartoons appearing in that chapter were drawn by Professor Chisholm. The preliminary discussion of Chapter 4 was inspired by J. G. Fichte's *The*

V*ocation of Man,* and the expression "soft determinism," used in that chapter, is borrowed from William James's essay, "The Dilemma of Determinism." The "theory of agency" sketched in that chapter is more or less my own creation. It has been set forth more fully in my contribution to *Determinism and Freedom in the Age of Modern Science,* a symposium edited by Sidney Hook, published by the New York University Press (1958). The version of the argument from design given in Chapter 7 was derived from a discussion with Dr. James Kiefer, a mathematician whom I met only once, and who on that occasion convinced me of the merit of this argument. He in turn, I believe, got the argument from C. S. Lewis, though I have been unable to verify this. The central argument in Chapter 5 is taken, with revisions and, I hope, improvements, from my paper "Fatalism," which appeared in *The Philosophical Review,* Vol. 71, 1962. The introductory part of Chapter 6 was partly derived from my paper "Spatial and Temporal Analogies and the Concept of Identity," in *The Journal of Philosophy,* Vol. 52, 1955. The original version of that paper was inspired throughout by the concluding chapter of Nelson Goodman's *The Structure of Appearance* and my indebtedness to this author is enormous. Part of the remainder of that chapter is derived from my "Pure Becoming," which appeared in *The Australasian Journal of Philosophy,* Vol. 38, 1960. I hereby express my thanks to the editors of these journals for permission to use this material. I wish also to express my gratitude to Brown University for a summer grant that provided me with the leisure to compose this book.

RICHARD TAYLOR

CONTENTS

Metaphysics

INTRODUCTION

It is sometimes said that everyone has a philosophy and even that all men have metaphysical views. Nothing could be sillier. It is true that all men have opinions, and that some of these—such as views on religion, morals, and the meaning of life—border on philosophy and metaphysics, but few men have any conception of philosophy, and fewer still any notion of metaphysics.

William James somewhere defined metaphysics as "nothing but an unusually obstinate effort to think clearly." Not many people think like this, except where their practical interests are involved. There is no need for them to do so, and hence, no inclination. Except for rare, reflective souls, men go through life just taking for granted those questions of existence, purpose, and meaning that the metaphysician finds most puzzling. What first of all claims the attention of all creatures, and of all men, is the need to survive and, this being once reasonably assured, the need to exist as securely as possible. All thought begins there, and most of it ends there. We are most at home when thinking of *how* to do this or that. Hence engineering, politics, and industry are quite natural to men. But metaphysics is concerned not at all with the hows of life, but only with the whys, with questions that it is perfectly easy never to ask in one's whole lifetime.

To think metaphysically is to think, without arbitrariness and dogmatism, on the most basic problems of existence. The problems are basic in the sense that they are fundamental, that much depends on them. Religion, for example, is not metaphysics; and yet if the metaphysical theory of materialism should be true, and it should thus be a fact that men have no souls, then much religion would founder on that fact. Again, moral philosophy is not metaphysics, and yet if the metaphysical theory of determinism should be true, or if the theory of fatalism should be true, many of our traditional presuppositions of morality would stand refuted by those truths. Similarly, logic is not metaphysics, and yet if it should turn out that, because of the nature of time, some assertions are neither true nor false, this would have serious implications for traditional logic.

This suggests, contrary to what is widely assumed, that metaphysics is a foundation of philosophy, and not its capstone. One's philosophical thinking, if long pursued, tends to resolve itself into basic problems of metaphysics. This is why metaphysical thought is difficult. Indeed, it would probably be true to say that the fruit of metaphysical thought is not knowledge but understanding. Metaphysical questions have answers, and among competing answers, not all, certainly, can be true. If one man asserts a theory of materialism and another denies that theory, then one of those men is in error; and so it is with every other metaphysical theory. Yet it can very seldom be proved and known which theory is true. Understanding, however—and sometimes a very considerable depth of it—results from seeing the obstinate difficulties in views which often seem, on other grounds, quite obviously true. It is for this reason that a man can be a wise metaphysician who nevertheless suspends his judgment on metaphysical views. Such a man can see all that the metaphysical dogmatist sees, and can see all the reasons for asserting what another man asserts with such confidence. But unlike that other, he sees also some reasons for doubting, and thus he is, like Socrates, the wiser, even in his profession of ignorance. Let the reader be warned, accordingly, that whenever he hears a philosopher proclaim any metaphysical opinion with great confidence, or hears him assert that something in metaphysics is obvious, or that some metaphysical problem turns only on confusions of concepts or upon the meanings of words, then he can be quite sure that this man is still infinitely far from philosophical understanding. His views appear to him devoid of difficulties only because he stoutly refuses to see difficulties.

A metaphysical problem is inseparable from its data, for it is these that give rise to the problem in the first place. Now "datum" means, literally, something *given*. Thus, we take as the data of a problem certain elementary beliefs of common sense which all or most men are apt to hold with some conviction prior to philosophical reflection, and which they would be reluctant to abandon. They are not themselves philosophical theories, for these are the product of philosophical reflection and usually result from the attempt to reconcile certain data with each other. They are instead the starting points for theories, the things we begin with; for in order to do anything at all, we must begin with something, and cannot spend forever just getting started. "To seek proof of matters for which we already possess clearer evidence than any proof can afford," Aristotle noted, "is to confuse the better with the worse, the plausible with the implausible, and the basic with the deriva-tive" (*Physics*, Bk. VIII, Ch. 3). Examples of metaphysical data are the beliefs almost every man has, independent of philosophy, that he exists, that he has a body, that past things are no longer within his control, that he sometimes has a choice between alternative courses of action, that he sometimes deliberates on these, that he is growing older and will someday die, and so on. A metaphysical *problem* arises when it is found that such data do not all seem to agree with each other, that they appear to have implications which are inconsistent with each other. The task then is to find some theory that is adequate to remove these conflicts.

It should perhaps be noted that data, as I am considering them, are not things that are necessarily true, nor are they self-evident. In fact, if the conflict between certain of one's common-sense beliefs is not merely apparent but real, then some of those beliefs are bound to be false, though they might nevertheless count as data until their falsity is discovered. It is this that makes metaphysics sometimes exciting; namely, that one is sometimes driven to abandon certain opinions that he had always deemed quite obvious. Nevertheless, metaphysics has to begin with something, and since it obviously cannot *begin* with things that are proved, it must begin with things that are believed; and the confidence with which one holds his metaphysical theories can be no greater than the confidence he reposes in the data upon which they rest.

Now the intellects of men are not as strong as their wills, and men generally believe whatever they want to believe, particularly when those beliefs reflect upon their own worth among men and the value of their endeavors. *Wisdom* is thus not what men first of all seek. They seek, instead, the justification for what they happen to cherish. It is not surprising, then, that beginners in philosophy, and even those who are not beginners, have a strong inclination to hold fast to some theory that appeals to them, in the face of conflicting data, and sometimes to deny that the data are true just for this reason. This hardly promotes wisdom. Thus, it is not uncommon to find someone who, say, wants badly to believe in the theory of determinism, and who from this de-sire simply denies the truth of any data that conflict with it. The data, in other words, are simply adjusted to the theory, rather than the theory to the data. But it must still be insisted that it is the data, and not the theory, that one should begin with; for if we do not begin with some fairly plausible presuppositions, where are we going to get the theory, other than just embracing what our hearts desire? We may sooner or later have to abandon some of our common-sense data, but when we do, it should be in deference to certain other common-sense beliefs which we are even more reluctant to relinquish, and not in deference to philosophical theories which are appealing.

The reader is therefore exhorted, in pursuing the thoughts that follow, to suspend his judgment concerning the final truths of things, since probably neither he nor anyone else knows what these are, and to content himself with appreciating the problems of metaphysics. This is the first and always the most difficult step. The rest of the truth, if he is ever blessed to receive any of it, will come from within him, if it ever comes at all, and not from the reading of books.

The discussion that follows constitutes an introduction—literally, a "leading in"—to metaphysics. It is not a survey of prevailing views, and the reader will search in vain for the names of great thinkers or summaries of opinions they held. Metaphysical problems are elicited, and the reader is simply invited to think on them along the lines suggested. It is for this reason that, in developing problems most closely associated with the *self* or *person* and its powers, particularly in the first three chapters, the stylistically objectionable first person singular "I" is frequently employed, after the manner of Descartes' *Meditations*. The reader should understand that the ideas presented in this form are intended as his own, and not as autobiographical reflections of the author.

PERSONS AND BODIES

1

Sometimes the simplest and most obvious distinctions give rise to the profoundest intellectual difficulties, and things most commonplace in our daily experience drive home to us the depths of our ignorance. Men have fairly well fathomed the heavens, so that perhaps nothing counts as surer knowledge than astronomy, the science of the things most distant from us, and yet the grass at our feet presents impenetrable mysteries. In like manner, our knowledge of man, of human history, of cultures remote in time and distance, fills volumes, and yet each of us is bewildered by that one being that is closest to him, namely, himself, as soon as he asks the most elementary questions. And oddly, it seems that the simplest question one can ask about himself—the question namely, What am I?—is the very hardest to answer, and nonetheless the most important. One can ask of many other things, including some very complex ones—such as a tree, a drop of water, or a machine—just what they are, and be quite certain that his answers, though incomplete, are nonetheless not wholly wrong. But when one asks what he himself is, what he is in his innermost nature; when he asks what is that "I" with which he is so intimately concerned and which is for him the very center of the universe, then he is bewildered, and must fall back on philosophical speculations of the most difficult sort.

It is, moreover, this simple and basic question that has the greatest philosophical ramifications. All morals, religion, metaphysics, and law turn upon it. Law and morality, for example, presuppose the existence of moral agents who have responsibilities and are capable of incurring guilt. But obviously, certain kinds of things can have responsibilities, and certain others cannot; and if men are in fact beings of the latter kind, then morality and law, as traditionally conceived, are nonsense. Again, many religions presuppose that men are spiritual beings, capable of surviving the destruction of their bodies in death. If a man is in fact nothing of the sort, then those religions rest upon a misconception. It is thus imperative that we try to find some answer to this basic and simple question.

Now while most men are, throughout their lives, almost wholly absorbed in practical ends, in the pursuit of the objects of their desires, so that their thoughts are perpetually directed to outward things, a reflective man is nonetheless sometimes led to consider his own being, which is then apt to seem to him mysterious. Thus, when someone dies, who was well known and perhaps loved, it is quite natural to think that this person is not the same thing as those remains that sink into the grave, for it is not these that were so known and loved. A religious man in these circumstances is therefore apt to speak, not of death, but of departing. Again, when one rejoices over his achievements, particularly if they seem to have some profound moral significance, or when he repents of his failures, he is not likely to suppose that his body, or any part of it, such as his nervous system, is the object of such attitudes. Instead, it is that in him which makes him distinctively *personal*, for he congratulates or reproaches *himself*. And so it is with all distinctively human relations, like love and friendship, which seem to unite persons, and not simply natural physical bodies such as are the subject matter of physical science.

The reality of the self and the body However unsure I may be of the nature of myself and of the relation of myself to my body, I can hardly doubt the reality of either. Whether I am identical with my body, or whether I am a spirit, or soul, or perhaps only a collection of thoughts and feelings— whatever I am, I cannot doubt my own being, cannot doubt that I am part of the world, even prior to any philosophical reflection on the matter. For surely if I know anything at all, as presumably I do, then I know that I exist. There seems to be nothing I could possibly know any better. And this is, of course, quite consistent with my great ignorance as to the nature of that self of whose existence I feel so assured.

I know, further, that I have a body. I may have learned this from experience, in the same way that I have learned of the existence of innumerable other things, or I may not have; it is, in any case, something I surely know. I may also have only the vaguest conception, or even a totally erroneous one, of the relationship between myself and my body; I can nevertheless no more doubt the reality of the one than the other. I may also be, as I surely am, quite ignorant of the nature and workings of my body and even of many of its parts, but no such ignorance raises the slightest doubt of its reality.

Now what is the connection between these, between myself and my body? Just what relationship am I affirming by "have," when I say with such confidence that I have a body? Abstractly, there seem to be just three general possibilities. In the first place, my having a body might consist simply in the *identity* of myself with my body, or of my *being* a body. Or second, it might amount to *possession*, such that my having a body consists essentially in this body's being among the various other things that I own or possess, it being at the same time, perhaps, in some way unique among these. Or finally, there may be some special, perhaps highly metaphysical relationship between the two, such as that I as a person am one thing, my body another quite different thing, the two being somehow connected to each other in a special way, appropriately expressed by the assertion that the one *has* the other.

Now there are great difficulties in all these suggestions, and, under the third, numerous special theories are possible, as we shall see. We had best, however, begin with the simplest view, to see then whether any of the others are any better.

Materialism   I know that I have a body, and that this is a material thing, though a somewhat unusual and highly complicated one. There would, in fact, be no other reason for calling it my body, except to affirm that it is entirely material, for nothing that is not matter could possibly be a part of my body. Now if my having a body consists simply in the identity of myself with my body, then it follows that I *am* a body, and nothing more. Nor would the affirmation of the identity of myself with my body be at all inconsistent with saying that I have a body, for we often express the relationship of identity in just this way. Thus, one might correctly say of a table that it *has* four legs and a top, or of a bicycle that it *has* two wheels, a frame, a seat, and handle bars. In such cases, no one would suppose that the table or the bicycle is one thing, and its parts or "body" another, the two being somehow mysteriously connected. The table or the bicycle just *is* its parts, suitably related. So likewise, I might just *be* the totality of my bodily parts, suitably related and all functioning together in the manner expressed by saying that I am a living body, or a living, material animal organism.

This materialistic conception of a person has the great advantage of simplicity. We do know that there are bodies, that there are living animal bodies, and that some of these are in common speech denominated men. A person is, then, on this view, nothing mysterious or metaphysical, at least as regards the *kind* of thing he is.

A consequence of this simplicity is that we need not speculate upon the relationship between one's body and his mind, or ask how the two are connected, or how one can act upon the other, all such questions being rendered senseless within the framework of this view, which in the first place denies that we are dealing with two things. The death of the animal organism—which is, of course, an empirical fact and not subject to speculation—will, moreover, be equivalent to the destruction of the person, consisting simply in the cessation of those functions which together constitute being alive. Hence, the fate of a person is simply, on this view, the fate of his body, which is ultimately a return to the dust whence he sprang. This alleged identity of oneself with his body accounts, moreover, for the solicitude every man has for his body, and for its health and well-being. If a person is identical with his body, then any threat to the latter is a threat to himself, and he must view the destruction of it as the destruction of himself. And such, in fact, does seem to be the attitude of all men, whatever may be their philosophical or religious opinions. Again, the distinction that every man draws between himself and other persons, or himself and other things, need be no more than the distinction between one body and others. When I declare that some foreign object—a doorknob, for instance, or a shoe—is no part of myself, I may be merely making the point that it is no part of my body. I would, surely, be more hesitant in declaring that my hand, or my brain and nervous system, which are physical objects, are no parts of me.

Such a conception has nevertheless always presented enormous difficulties, and these have seemed so grave to most philosophers that almost any theory, however absurd when examined closely, has at one time or another seemed to them preferable to materialism. Indeed, the difficulties of materialism are so grave that, for some persons, they need only to be mentioned to render the theory unworthy of discussion.

The meaning of "identity"   By "identity" the materialist must mean a strict and total identity of himself and his body, nothing less. Now to say of anything, X, and anything, Y, that X and Y are identical, or that they are really one and the same thing, one must be willing to assert of X anything whatever that he asserts of Y, and vice versa. This is simply a consequence of their identity, for if there is anything whatever that can be truly asserted of any object X, but cannot be truly asserted of some object Y, then it logically follows that X and Y are two different things, and not the same thing. In saying, for instance, that the British wartime prime minister and Winston Churchill are one and the same person, one commits himself to saying of either whatever he is willing to say of the other—such as, that he lived to a great age, smoked cigars, was a resolute leader, was born at Blenheim, and so on. If there were any statement whatever that was true of, say, Mr. Churchill, but not true of the wartime prime minister, then it would follow that Mr. Churchill was not the wartime prime minister, that we are here referring to two different men, and not one.

The question can now be asked, then, whether there is anything true of me that is not true of my body, and vice versa. There are, of course, ever so many things that can be asserted indifferently of both me and my body without absurdity. For instance, we can say that I was born at such and such place and time, and it is not the least odd to say this of my body as well. Or we can say that my body now weighs exactly so many pounds, and it would be just as correct to give this as my weight; and so on.

But now consider more problematical assertions. It might, for instance, be true of me at a certain time that I am morally blameworthy or praiseworthy. Can we then say that my body or some part of it, such as my brain, is in exactly the same sense blameworthy or praiseworthy? Can moral predicates be applied without gross incongruity to any physical object at all? Or suppose I have some profound wish or desire, or some thought—the desire, say, to be in some foreign land at a given moment, or thoughts of the Homeric gods. It seems at least odd to assert that my body, or some part of it, wishes that it were elsewhere, or has thoughts of the gods. How, indeed, can any purely physical state of any purely physical object ever be a state that is *for* something, or *of* something, in the way that my desires and thoughts are such? And how, in particular, could a purely physical state be in this sense *for* or *of* something that is not real? Or again, suppose that I am religious, and can truly say that I love God and neighbor, for instance. Can I without absurdity say that my body or some part of it, such as my foot or brain, is religious, and loves God and neighbor? Or can one suppose that my being religious, or having such love, consists simply in my body's being in a certain state, or behaving in a certain way? If I claim the identity of myself with my body, I must say all these odd things; that is, I must be willing to assert of my body, or some part of it, everything I assert of myself. There is perhaps no logical absurdity or clear falsity in speaking thus of one's corporeal frame, but such assertions as these are at least strange, and it can be questioned whether, as applied to the body, they are even still meaningful.

The disparity between bodily and personal predicates becomes even more apparent, however, if we consider epistemological predicates, involved in statements about belief and knowledge. Thus, if I believe something—believe, for instance, that today is February 31—then I am in a certain state; the state, namely, of having a certain belief which is in this case necessarily a false one. Now how can a physical state of any physical object be identical with that? And how, in particular, can anything be a *false* physical state of an object? The physical states of things, it would seem, just *are*, and one cannot even think of anything that could ever distinguish one such state from another as being either true or false. A physiologist might give a complete physical description of a brain and nervous system at a particular time, but he could never distinguish some of those states as true and others as false, nor would he have any idea what to look for if he were asked to do this. At least, so it would certainly seem.

Platonic dualism   It is this sort of reflection that has always led metaphysicians and theologians to distinguish radically between the mind or soul of a man and his body, ascribing properties to the mind that are utterly different in kind from those exhibited by the body; properties which, it is supposed, could not be possessed by any body, just because of its nature as a physical object.

The simplest and most radical of such views *identifies* the person or self with a soul or mind, and declares its relationship to the body to be the almost accidental one of mere occupancy, possession, or use. Thus Plato, and many mystical philosophers before and after him, thought of the body as a veritable prison of the soul, a gross thing of clay from which the soul one day gladly escapes, to live its own independent and untrammeled existence, much as a bird flees its cage or a snake sheds its skin. A person, thus conceived, is a non-material substance—a *spirit*, in the strictest sense—related to an animal body as possessor to thing possessed, tenant to abode, or user to thing used. A person *has* a body only in the sense that he, perhaps temporarily, occupies, owns, or uses a body, being all the while something quite distinct from it and having, perhaps, a destiny quite different from the melancholy one that is known sooner or later to overtake the corporeal frame.

This dualism of mind and body has been, and always is, firmly received by millions of unthinking men, partly because it is congenial to the religious framework in which their everyday metaphysical opinions are formed, and partly, no doubt, because every man wishes to think of himself as something more than just one more item of matter in the world. Wise philosophers, too, speak easily of the attributes of the mind as distinct from those of the body, thereby sundering the two once and for all. Some form of dualism seems in fact indicated by the metaphysical, moral, and epistemological difficulties of materialism which are, it must be confessed, formidable indeed.

But whatever difficulties such simple dualism may resolve, it appears to raise others equally grave. For one thing, it is not nearly as simple as it seems. Whatever a partisan of such a view might say of the simplicity of the mind or soul, a *man* is nonetheless, on this view, *two* quite disparate things, a mind and a body, having almost nothing in common and only the flimsiest connection with each other. This difficulty, once it is acutely felt, is usually minimized by conceiving of a man, in his true self as nothing but a mind, and representing his body as something ancillary to this true self, something that is not really any part of him at all but only one among the many physical objects that he happens to possess, use, or what not, much as he possesses and uses various other things in life. His body does, to be sure, occupy a preeminent place among such things, for it is something without which he would be quite helpless; but this renders it no more a part or whole of his true self or person than any other of the world's physical things.

Possession, however, is essentially a social concept, and sometimes a strictly legal one. Something counts as one of my possessions by virtue of my title to it, and this is something conferred by men, in accordance with conventions and laws fabricated by men themselves. Thus does a field or a building count as one of my possessions. But a certain animal body, which I identify as mine, is not mine in any sense such as this. My dominion over my body arises from no human conventions or laws, and is not alterable by them. The body of a slave, though it may be owned by another man in the fullest sense of ownership that is reflected in the idea of possession, is nevertheless the slave's body in a metaphysical sense in which it could not possibly be the body of his master. One has, moreover, a solicitude for his body wholly incommensurate with his concern for any treasure, however dear. The loss of the latter is regarded as no more than a loss, though perhaps a grave one, while the abolition of one's body cannot be regarded as the mere loss of something dearly held, but is contemplated by any man as an appalling and total calamity.

The ideas of occupancy or use do not express the relation of mind and body any better. *Occupancy*, for instance, is a physical concept; one thing occupies another by being in or upon it. But the mind, on this view, is no physical thing, and no sense can be attached to its resting within or upon any body; the conception is simply ridiculous. Nor does one simply *use* his body the way he uses implements and tools. One does, to be sure, sometimes use his limbs and other parts, over which he has voluntary control, in somewhat the manner in which he uses tools; but many of one's bodily parts, including some that are vital, the very existence of which may be unknown to him, are not within his control at all. They are nonetheless parts of his body. Artificial devices, too, like hearing aids, spectacles, and the like, do not in the least become parts of one's body merely by being used, even in the case of a man who can barely do without them. They are merely things worn or used. Nor can one say that one's body is that physical being in the world upon which one absolutely depends for his continuing life, for there are many such things. One depends on the sun, for instance, and the air he breathes; without these would perish as certainly as if deprived of his heart; yet no one regards the sun or the air around him as any part of his body.

A man does not, then, *have* a body in the way in which he has anything else at all, and any comparison of the body to a material possession or instrument is about as misleading as likening it to a chamber in which one is more or less temporarily closeted. The connection between oneself and his body is far more intimate and metaphysical than anything else we can think of. One's body is at least a part of himself, and is so regarded by every man. Yet it is not merely a part, as the arm is part of the body; and we are so far without any hint of how the mind and the body are connected.

A plethora of   Clearly, if one so much as *distinguishes* between his body and his
theories   mind, and treats these as two different things, he raises problems
              of such enormous difficulty that any theory, however bizarre, is apt to appear plausible if it offers some hope of removing them. Just once sunder body and mind, and enough problems are created to keep philosophers at work for generations. There is, in fact, hardly any theory so bizarre that it has not at one time or another found strong defenders among the most able thinkers. Just as materialists, for example, in the effort to obviate the necessity of connecting mind and matter, have simply denied the existence of minds, so also have *idealists* denied the existence of matter, maintaining that all bodies, including one's own, exist only as ideas in some mind. Others, unwilling to deny the existence either of minds or of bodies, have suggested that the connection between them is that of cause and effect, that my body acts upon my mind and my mind upon my body, and that just this causality is what connects and unites the two into one person. This is the theory of *interactionism*. Others, unable to see how a mind, which is not material, can have physical effects, have maintained that the body acts upon the mind to produce consciousness, thought, and feeling, but that the mind itself has no physical effects, which is the theory of *epiphenomenalism*. Still others, finding the same difficulty in the idea of the body's acting upon the mind as in the idea of the mind's acting upon the body, have suggested that there is really only one kind of substance, and that what we call "mind" and "body" are simply two aspects of this. This is called the *double aspect* theory. Again, to meet the same difficulty, it has been supposed that mind and body, being different substances, never act upon each other, but the histories of each are

nevertheless such that there *seems* to be such a causal connection. This is the theory of *parallelism*. It has even been suggested that this parallelism is wrought by God, who, in creating a person, arranges in advance that his mental and physical histories should always be in close correspondence without interacting, in the manner of a *pre-established harmony*. Alternatively, it has been seriously maintained that all of one's mental life is caused, from moment to moment, by God, who sees to it that this mental life is in close correspondence with what is going on in the body. This theory has come down to us under the name of *occasionalism*.

Most of these theories are not deserving of serious attention, but they are mentioned to give some intimation of the difficulty of our problem. A seemingly outrageous theory can cease to seem outrageous if the difficulties it promises to remove are enormous ones, and worth almost any price to get rid of. Of all these theories we shall in the next chapters consider only those of interactionism and epiphenomenalism, which are the only ones that are now widely maintained, except for materialism, to which we shall then return. Meanwhile, the theories just mentioned are graphically compared in the accompanying illustrations (p. 13).

INTERACTIONISM

2

Since I can hardly deny that I exist, and that I have a body which is at least a part of myself, then I must either affirm the identity of myself with my body, according to the materialistic conception described earlier, or else affirm that I am two things—a mind that has a body and, equally, a body that has a mind. Nothing else is consistent with the data with which we began.

Now the simplest and commonest way of expressing the relation between a body and a mind, so that they together constitute a person, is to say that they interact; that is, they causally act, each upon the other. More fully we can say that while the mind of a person is not a physical thing, events that transpire within it sometimes have causal consequences or effects within the body. Conversely, while the body of a person is clearly not a mental or nonphysical thing, the events that occur within it, particularly within the nervous system and brain, sometimes have causal consequences or effects within the mind or consciousness. The body and mind of an individual man, accordingly, are whatever body and mind are so related. My body is that physical object that is within my immediate control, that is, that physical object, alone, among all the others in the universe, that events within my mind are capable of affecting directly; and similarly, my mind is that mind, among all the others in the universe, that events within my body are capable of affecting directly. This, according to the view we are now considering, is what is meant by saying of a given body that it is mine, or that I have a certain body. What I am, accordingly, is a certain composite of body and mind that thus interact with each other.

Now this conception of a person, which is very old and familiar, appears in some measure confirmed by the manner in which we often describe certain of our experiences. Thus, when there is some disorder in my body, such as a severely decayed tooth, or a laceration in the skin, it appears clearly to be the *cause* of a purely subjective, unobservable state called *pain*. And the fact that such a pain is subjective and unobservable to anyone else suggests that it is not, like the decay or the laceration, a state of my body at all, but rather something mental. Thus, a dentist can observe the decay, and a physiologist can describe in some detail the changes within my nerves, which are further bodily changes, that this decay gives rise to; but both the dentist and physiologist are necessarily barred from ever observing the pain that is the ultimate effect of these bodily changes, just because it is not, like these, a bodily change at all. Instruments of increasing refinement, such as microscopes and the like, can pick out more and more bodily changes, hitherto unobserved. Their inability ever to pick out a pain for observation does not result from their inadequacy as instruments of observation, but from metaphysical considerations. A pain cannot, along with physical changes of whatever minuteness, be observed by any devices whatsoever, simply because it is not a physical change at all but a mental one, and for that reason unobservable. The only person who can become aware of a pain or any other state of mind or mental event is that person in whose mind it occurs, and his awareness of it is, of course, immediate. Even he cannot observe it in the same way that he observes any physical object, state, or change, whether in his own body or some other.

Similarly, it is not uncommon to think of purely mental changes having observable effects within the body. Fear, for example, is a subjective, mental state that produces visible perspiration and other bodily changes. Again, the mere thought of food sometimes produces salivation, and some persons' hands can be made to perspire by the mere thought of high places and other precarious situations. Voluntary activity, moreover, is often represented as bodily behavior having among its causes one's choices, decisions, intentions, or volitions, and these are psychological in nature and hence unobservable by any outsider. Though someone were able to witness *all* the inner and outer workings of my body, in all its minutest parts, and accurately describe *all* the physical and chemical changes occurring therein, he could not, it is often alleged, ever pick out one of my volitions or choices. He could see the *effects* of these in the form of gross and subtle bodily changes; but he could not see the choices or volitions that cause these effects, simply because they are *not* bodily changes to begin with. They are changes within the mind, and for that reason metaphysically incapable of being observed.

However natural it may seem to conceive a person in such terms, as a dual complex of two wholly disparate things, body and mind, it is nonetheless an impossible conception, on the simplest metaphysical grounds. For on this view, the body and the mind *are* wholly disparate things, so that any bodily change, wrought by the mind or by some nonphysical occurrence transpiring therein, is a change that lies quite outside the realm of physical law. This means that human behavior is veritably miraculous. Now some persons, reflecting on the old dictum that anything, after all, can cause anything, might be willing to accept this consequence, thus broadly stated, pointing out at the same time that human nature is, after all, somewhat mysterious. Nevertheless, when we come to some precise instance of the alleged interaction of body and mind, as conceived by this theory, we find that we are dealing with something that is not merely mysterious but wholly unintelligible.

Consider some clear and simple case of what would on this theory constitute the action of the mind upon the body. Suppose, for example, that I am dwelling in my thought upon high and precarious places, all the while knowing that I am really safely ensconced in my armchair. I imagine, perhaps, that I am picking my way along a precipice, and visualize the destruction that awaits me far below in case I make the smallest slip. Soon, simply as the result of these thoughts and images, which are not for a moment attended by any belief that I am in the slightest danger, perspiration appears on the palms of my hands. Now here is surely a case, if there is any, of something purely mental, unobservable, and wholly outside the realm of physical nature, bringing about observable physical changes. We do not have in this situation an instance of physical stimuli from the environment causing physical reactions in the organism, for the actual stimuli are the normal ones of my room and armchair, and these do not change. The only significant change is in my thoughts and images, which are directly in the control of my will and are followed by the physical effect on my hands. Here, then, one wants to say, the mind acts upon the body, producing perspiration.

But what actually happens, alas, is not nearly so simple as this. To say that thoughts in the mind produce sweat on the hands is to simplify the situation so grossly as hardly approximate to any truth at all of what actually happens. A complete account of the complexities involved here cannot be given, for it is unknown, but some elaboration is possible, in the light of which it is far from obvious that we have, even in this case, an instance of the mind acting on the body.

The perspiration, everyone knows, is secreted by tiny but complex little glands in the skin. They are caused to secrete this substance, not by any mind acting on them, but by the contraction of little unstriated muscles. These tiny muscles are composed of numerous minute cells, wherein occur chemical reactions of the most baffling complexity. It is believed, however, that the energy required for their activity is derived from the oxidation of fatty acids, or perhaps of acetoacetate. Their contraction in any case generates electrical current of small but measurable amounts. It might be supposed that these muscles are innervated by the mind, which by some mysterious alchemy produces the chemical reactions within their cells; but this, even if it makes any sense, is certainly not true. The muscles are activated by hormones produced by the adrenal medulla in response to impulses of the autonomic nervous system, probably by the hormones epinephrine or norepinephrine or, more likely in the present case, by an epinephrine-like substance that is produced in minute quantities by adrenergic fibers, that is, certain postganglionic neurons of the sympathetic nervous system. Where this substance originally comes from is apparently not known, but it cannot be doubted that it is a physical substance—indeed, its chemical formula is known—and that it is synthesized in the body. It has, in any case, no mental or extraphysical origin. Now it is the activity of the neurons of the sympathetic nervous system that leads to the production of this epinephrine-like substance by the adrenergic fibers. How impulses are propagated by these neurons is also not entirely understood, but it seems to be somewhat as follows. Stimulation of a neuron increases the permeability of the neuron membrane, causing a diffusion of sodium ions into the neuron itself, so that the neuron within becomes positively charged with respect to the outside, with a resultant flow of current. Such currents are easily detected and fairly accurately measured by a physiologist. The diffused fibers of the sympathetic nervous system coalesce and center about two chains of ganglia which are arranged along the sides of the spinal cord. Unlike the neurons of the parasympathetic nervous system, those of the sympathetic nervous system synapse near these ganglia. The nerve impulse is transmitted across the synapse by the help of acetylcholine, a fairly well-known substance which is believed to be produced by the terminal fibrils of the nerves. The cells of the spinal ganglia are supplied by preganglionic neuron fibers arising from the spinal cord. These, in turn, connect eventually, and in the most dreadfully complicated way, with the hypothalamus, a delicate part of the brain that is centrally involved in the emotional reactions of the organism, and in the so-called homeostasis of the organism; i.e., in the self-regulation of its internal environment. How it operates to effect this internal balance, and to originate those impulses that lead to such diverse effects as sweating, increased pulse, and so on, is quite unclear, but it is not seriously considered by those who do know something about it that mental events must be included in the description of its operations. The hypothalamus, in turn, is closely connected with the cortex and subcortical areas of the brain, so that physical and chemical changes within these areas produce responding physical effects within the hypothalamus, which in turn, by a series of physical processes whose complexity has only barely been suggested, produces such remote effects as the secretion of perspiration on the surface of the hands.

Such, in the barest outline, is something of the chemistry and physics of emotional perspiration. What is involved is an enormously complex causal chain of physical processes. For each part of this causal chain that is understood, there are doubtless a hundred that are not. The important point, however, is that in describing it as best we can, there is no need, at any stage, to introduce mental or nonphysical substances or reactions. The diffusion of sodium ions into a neuron, for instance, with the resultant flow of current, is not perfectly understood, but no one supposes that the understanding of this would be enhanced by reference to nonphysical or mental events, nor is it even possible to imagine how such nonphysical events could ever bring about, abet, or inhibit any such ion diffusion.

We know the end result of this chain of physical processes; it is the secretion of perspiration on the hands. We know, more or less, a good many of the intermediate processes. The baffling question that now arises, however, is how such a complex series gets *started*. The hypothalamus, we noted, is closely connected with the cortex and subcortical parts of the brain. Presumably, then, it is some change within these that eventuates, finally, in the secretion of perspiration. The brain, however, is a physical object, and the only changes it is capable of undergoing are physical changes, similar to those manifested in any other part of the body. If, accordingly, the mind acts upon the body to produce perspiration on the hands, it is here, in the cortex or subcortical parts of the brain, that such interaction occurs.

But how exactly are we to conceive of this action of the mind · upon that portion of the brain? Presumably thoughts, that is, ideas or images, occur "within the mind." This must not for a moment be understood to mean that these occur within the brain or any part of it, for they are, according to the view we have been considering, strictly nonphysical entities having no location in space, either within the head or elsewhere, and no physical property whatever that would ever render them susceptible to observation or even to any detection by microscopes, probes, or any other physical apparatus. Yet these nonphysical things do, according to this view, act upon a physical object, the brain. What we must conceive, then, is a physical change within the brain, this change being wrought, not by some other physical change in the brain or elsewhere, but by an *idea*. We do not know what that physical change in the brain is, but that does not matter so long as it is clearly understood that it is a change of a physical substance, the brain. We can suppose, then, just to get some sort of picture before us, that it is a change consisting of the diffusion of sodium ions into certain of the brain's cells. Conceive, then, if possible, how an *idea* can effect such a change as this, how an idea can render more permeable the membranes of certain brain cells, or how an idea can enter into a chemical reaction whose effect is the diffusion of sodium ions at a certain place, how an idea can move the particles of the cortical cells or otherwise aid or inhibit chemical reactions occurring therein. Try, I say, to form a conception of this, and then confess that, as soon as the smallest attempt at any description is made, the description becomes unintelligible and the conception an impossible one. That compounds should be constituted and decomposed by physical forces and according to physical law, that minute particles of matter should be moved hither or thither by the action upon them of other particles, that a substance should be ionized by an electrical current or by the action of another physical substance—all this is clearly intelligible. But that these same things should be made to happen without any physical substances or physical processes among their causal antecedents, that they should be wrought by something so nebulous as an idea or mental image, by something having no physical property and not even a location, by something that could never enter into the physical description of anything, or into any chemical equation, and in violation of the very physical laws and principles according to which all physical objects such as the brain and its parts operate—that anything like this should happen seems quite unintelligible. It is one thing to say that the mind acts upon the body. But it is quite another thing to give some clear instance of a bodily change and then try to imagine how the mind, or any thought or idea, could in any way be involved in any such change as that. To say that a diffusion of sodium ions was caused by an "idea" is not to give any causal explanation at all. It is, rather, to confess that the explanation of that diffusion is simply not known. One can in such terms always verbally describe human behavior or the activity of the nerves and brain and glands, interlarding the explanation here and there with references to mental or nonphysical processes; but no one can possibly understand what is thus verbally set forth, or form the least conception of how such interaction between wholly disparate realms of being is at all possible.

The locus of interaction That has always been the main difficulty in any theory of the interaction of mind and body, and it is a difficulty that is hardly removed by such glib phrases as "anything can cause anything." Interactionism becomes quite unintelligible as soon as one endeavors to spell out, in some considerable detail, some bodily change, and then to show how mental or nonphysical processes can in any way be involved in such a change. It is not enough to say that the mind acts upon the body or that some particular mental thing, like an idea, acts upon some particular part of the body, such as the sweat glands. It is the precise *localization* of such activity that presents a great difficulty; as of course it must, since mental processes are, by the very description that is usually given of them, not localizable in the first place. It is sometimes suggested that the mind acts not simply on "the body," but on the *brain*, but this too is altogether too loose. We noted that the hypothalamus, which is so significantly involved in so many bodily changes, is connected in the most elaborate way with various parts of the entire cerebrospinal system. Now surely, the mind does not act directly upon the hypothalamus. The hypothalamus is acted upon by stimuli received from these other areas of the body. We must imagine it possible, then, to indicate exactly, in the case of any particular instance of alleged mind-body interaction, the locus of this interaction. In the example we were considering, for instance, we can hardly suppose that the entire cerebrospinal complex acts upon the hypothalamus to produce those changes that finally result in perspiration on the hands. It is surely some particular part of the brain, some fairly precise part of the cortex perhaps, from which the hypothalamus receives its impulses. What the interactionist must be willing to say, accordingly, is that, in this particular instance of the action of the mind on the body, the mind acts on the body at that particular spot in the cortex. It must at least be thinkable that the part of the cortex involved could be designated with exactness—as being, for instance, that part which is just so far, and in just such and such a direction, from the lobe of the right ear. Now the interactionist must say that it is there, at that spot, that the mind acts upon the body in this example, causing, at just that spot, a diffusion of sodium ions into those cortical cells. And this, surely, is something that no one can really seriously maintain. If sodium ions are diffused into these particular cortical cells, the cause of this is a physical process within the brain, not a mental process within something belonging to a wholly different realm of being. This sort of difficulty, it will be noted, repeats itself, no matter how far back and into what remote corners of the cortex we trace the physical processes involved. To say at any point in the description that "the mind acts upon the body" is not to explain anything, but rather just to spare oneself the task of pursuing the description of the chain of physical processes any farther.

THE MIND AS A FUNCTION

OF THE BODY

3

In response to difficulties of the sort we have considered, many thinkers and investigators, particularly those not trained in philosophy, have been eager to maintain that human beings or persons are physical objects having, of course, psychological powers and attributes which distinguish them from other kinds of physical objects, but that such psychological powers and attributes can be understood in terms of certain bodily functions, or even identified with these.

Epiphenomenalism   Many such views amount to some version of epiphenomenalism, according to which mental entities, such as thoughts, images, ideas, and feelings, never enter as causes into any physical processes, and hence never act upon the body or any part of it, yet are some-times, if not always, the effects of bodily processes, particularly those within the nervous system. Mind and body do not, then, on this view *inter*act, for no mental state or event ever causes any bodily one. Yet the body does act upon the "mind" in this sense, that some, if not all, psychological states or events are the direct or indirect effects of occurrences within the body, especially those within the brain and nerves.

If, then, we ask our original question, concerning what a person essentially is, the answer turns out on this view to be something like this: A person is a living physical body having a mind, the mind consisting, however, of nothing but a more or less continuous series of conscious or unconscious states and events, such as feelings, thoughts, images, and ideas, which are the effects but never the causes of bodily activity.

Such a view does indeed avoid the apparent absurdities of or-

22

dinary interactionism, but it involves additional difficulties no less appalling and, when clearly conceived, appears so bizarre a description of human nature as to make almost any alternative conception more acceptable. For in the first place, whatever difficulty there is in the idea of purely mental entities entering into physical chains of causation and altering, for instance, the direction and outcome of chemical reactions and mechanical processes, there is no less difficulty in the idea that purely physical chains of causation, involving chemical reactions and the like, should have effects that could in principle never enter into the physical description of anything. That bodily processes, in other words, should have nonbodily effects is no more comprehensible than that mental processes should have nonmental effects; causation in either direction is neither more nor less difficult to comprehend than in the other.

The alleged superfluity of thought To see just how odd is the conception of human behavior that results from this view, we need to note carefully just what it asserts. It asserts that all bodily processes are self-contained; that is, that no nonbodily state or event ever enters causally into any physical process. It follows, then, that all bodily behavior is caused by bodily processes alone, and that the mind, and all states and events transpiring therein, being only incidental by-products of these physical processes, are entirely superfluous so far as the understanding and explanation of human behavior is concerned. This means that it makes no difference, so far as human behavior is concerned, whether those mental states and events exist or not, that human behavior would be just what it is without them, since they in no way influence the direction or outcome of any state, process, or motion of the body. But this seems quite impossible to believe. We can, no doubt, suppose that the behavior of certain organisms such as plants and insects is nothing but the resultant of physical or chemical processes within them, and is entirely without conscious direction, but it is impossible to believe that a man's thoughts and ideas have no influence upon what he does. One can hardly suppose that a man's behavior would be no different even if his mental life were quite different or even nonexistent, or that even the whole of human history, with all its wars and political upheavals, would have been just what it has been even without all those thoughts and feelings which, on this theory, superfluously attended them. What a man does is sometimes quite obviously the more or less direct outcome of what he thinks, desires, plans, and intends. Some allegedly mental states, such as twinges of pain and the like, may indeed be the mere accompaniments and effects of bodily processes, having themselves no direct influence on bodily behavior, but it is difficult to believe that the entire mental life of a man is the mere accompaniment and effect of bodily processes, and that those bodily processes—i.e., the whole of that man's observable behavior—are altogether unaffected by them.

Now it might be suggested, in response to this kind of *reductio ad absurdum* of epiphenomenalism, that causes are impossible without their effects. Since thoughts, ideas and feelings, then, are the regular effects of bodily changes, these latter could not occur without them. Hence (it might be claimed) whereas such thoughts, ideas, and feelings in no way act as causes of bodily behavior, that behavior would nevertheless be impossible without them, and it is therefore false to suggest that, on this theory, a man's behavior would be no different even in the absence of those mental phenomena.

This line of thought does not, however, properly represent the epiphenomenalist position. For according to epiphenomenalism, mental states are not the effects of observable bodily behavior but of certain states of the brain and nervous system, a man's observable behavior, including his voluntary acts, being likewise the effects of those same or other states of the brain and nervous system. States of the brain and nervous system, accordingly, have two entirely different *kinds* of effects, effects in two entirely different realms, the mental and the physical. Now so long as certain brain and nervous states occur, then on this theory the observable bodily behavior which is the consequence of them is guaranteed, whether the attendant mental effects occur or not, and these latter need not therefore be taken into account at all in the explanation of human conduct. They are, then, superfluous, after all, human behavior being unaffected either by their presence or their absence. Now one can indeed say that without the mental states, those particular brain and nerve states which are their normal causes could not occur, since from the nonoccurrence of the effect we can infer the nonoccurrence of its cause. But from this we cannot conclude that those mental states are necessary for the occurrence of the observable behavior of men, for that behavior might well be the effect of other bodily states, including, of course, other states of the brain and nervous system, and must in any case be the effect of *some* state of the body, according to the epiphenomenalist view.

Materialism again   We have drawn no closer to an answer to our question but have, on the contrary, gotten progressively farther from it, each difficulty raising a new theory having more difficulties in it than the last. Perhaps the only sure conclusion we can draw is that human nature is mysterious. But this, however unsatisfactory, is nonetheless worth affirming, for certainly no one can hold any of the views we have outlined, or any of the numberless variations on them, entirely without embarrassment, unless he simply resolves to see no obstacles where they are nonetheless securely lodged.

One thing should by now seem quite plain, however, and that is that the difficulties of simple materialism are not overcome by any form of dualism. There is, therefore, no point in recommending dualism as an improvement over materialism. To assert that a man is both body *and* mind—that is, that he is two things rather than one—not only does not remove any problem involved in saying that he is one thing only, namely, a body, but introduces all the problems of describing the connection between those two things. We are led to conclude, then, that a metaphysical understanding of human nature must be sought within the framework of materialism, according to which a man is entirely identical with his body.

All forms of dualism arise from the alleged disparity between persons and physical objects. Men, it is rightly noted, are capable of thinking, believing, feeling, wishing, and so on; but bodies, it is claimed, are capable of none of these things, and the conclusion is drawn that men are not bodies. Yet it cannot be denied that men *have* bodies; hence, it is decided that a man, or a person, is a nonphysical entity, somehow more or less intimately related to a body. But here it is rarely noted that whatever difficulties there may be in applying personal and psychological predicates and descriptions to bodies, precisely the same difficulties are involved in applying such predicates and descriptions to *anything whatever*, including spirits or souls. If, for example, a philosopher reasons that a body cannot think, and thereby affirms that, since a person thinks, a person is a soul or spirit or mind rather than a body, we are entitled to ask how a spirit can think. For surely, if a spirit or soul can think, we can affirm that a body can do so; and if we are the asked *how* a body can think, our reply can be that it thinks in precisely the manner in which the dualist supposes a soul thinks. The difficulty of imagining how a body thinks is not in the least lessened by asserting that something else, which is not a body, thinks. And so it is with every other personal predicate or description. Whenever faced with the dualist's challenge to explain how a body can have desires, wishes, how it can deliberate, choose, repent, how it can be intelligent or stupid, virtuous or wicked, and so on, our reply can always be: The body can do these things, and be these things, in whatever manner one imagines the soul can do these things and be these things. For to repeat, the difficulty here is in seeing how *anything at all* can deliberate, choose, repent, think, be virtuous or wicked, and so on, and *that* difficulty is not removed but simply glossed over by the invention of some new thing, henceforth to be called the "mind" or "soul."

It becomes quite obvious what is the source of dualistic metaphysics when the dualist or soul philosopher is pressed for some description of the mind or soul. The mind or soul, it turns out in such descriptions, is just whatever it is that thinks, reasons, deliberates, chooses, feels, and so on. But the fact with which we began was that *men* think, reason, deliberate, choose, feel, and so on. And we do in fact have some fairly clear notion of what we mean by a man, for we think of an individual man as a being existing in space and time, having a certain height and weight—as a being, in short, having many things in common with other objects in space and time, and particularly with those that are living, i.e., with other animals. But the dualist, noting that a man is significantly different from other beings, insofar as he, unlike most of them, is capable of thinking, deliberating, choosing, and so on, suddenly asserts that it is not a man, as previously conceived, that does these things at all, but something else, namely, a mind or soul, or something that does not exist in space and time nor have any height and weight, nor have, in fact, any material properties at all. And then when we seek some understanding of what this mind or soul is, we find it simply described as a thing that thinks, deliberates, feels, and so on. But surely the proper inference should have been that men are like all other physical objects in some respects—e.g., in having size, mass, and location in space and time; that they are like some physical objects but unlike others in certain further respects—e.g., in being living, sentient, and so on; and like no other physical objects at all in still other respects—e.g., in being rational, deliberative, and so on. And of course none of this suggests that men are not physical objects, but rather that they are precisely physical objects, like other bodies in some ways, unlike many other bodies in other ways, and unlike any other bodies in still other respects.

The dualist or soul philosopher reasons that since men think, feel, desire, choose, and so on, and since such things cannot be asserted of bodies, then men are not bodies. Reasoning in this fashion, we are forced to the conclusion that men are not bodies—though it is a stubborn fact that men nevertheless *have* bodies. So the great problem then is to connect men, now conceived as souls or minds, to their bodies. But philosophically, it is just exactly as good to reason that, since men think, feel, desire, choose, etc., and since men are bodies— i.e., are living, animal organisms having the essential material attributes of weight, size, and so on—then *some* bodies think, feel, desire, choose, etc. This argument is just as good as the dualist's argument and does not lead us into a morass of problems concerning the connection between soul and body.

The source of
duulislic
theories
Why, then, does the dualist's argument have, and this one lack, such an initial plausibility? Why have so many philosophers been led into dualistic metaphysical views, on the basis of arguments apparently no stronger than other arguments having simpler conclusions but which are rarely even considered?

Part of the answer is perhaps that, when we form an idea of a *body* or a *physical object*, what is most likely to come to mind is not some man or animal but something much simpler, such as a stone or a marble. When we are then invited to consider whether a physical object might think, deliberate, choose, and the like, we are led to contemplate the evident absurdity of supposing things like *that* do such things, and thus we readily receive the claim that bodies cannot think, deliberate, choose, and the like, and the dualist extracts his conclusion. But suppose we began somewhat differently. Suppose we began with a consideration of two quite dissimilar physical objects—a living, animal body, of the kind commonly denominated "man," on the one hand, and a simple body, of the kind denominated "stone," on the other. Now let it be asked whether there is any absurdity in supposing that one of these things might be capable of thinking, deliberating, choosing, and the like. Here there is no absurdity at all in asserting that an object of the first kind might indeed have such capacities, but evidently not one of the second kind—from which we would conclude, not that men are not physical objects, but rather that they are physical objects which are significantly different from other physical objects, such as stones. And there is, of course, nothing the least astonishing in this.

But how, one may wonder, can a "mere physical object" have feelings? But here the answer should be: Why, if it is a physical object of a certain familiar kind, should it not have feelings? Suppose, for example, that it is a living body, like a frog or mouse, equipped with a complicated and living nervous system. Where is the absurdity in asserting that a "mere physical object" of this sort can feel? Evidently there is none. Hardly anyone would want to insist that beings of this sort—frogs and mice, for instance—must have souls to enable them to feel. It seems enough that they have complicated living nervous systems.

The same type of answer can be given if it is asked how a "mere physical object" can think. If we suppose that it is a physical object of a certain familiar kind, namely, a living body having the form and other visible attributes of a man, and possessed of an enormously complex living brain and nervous system—in short, that the object in question is a living human being—then there is no absurdity in supposing that this being thinks. Any argument purporting to show that such a being cannot think, and must therefore have a nonmaterial soul to do its thinking for it, would be just as good an argument to show that frogs and mice cannot feel, and must therefore have souls to do their feeling for them. The outcome of such philosophizing is just as good, and just as absurd, in the one case as it is in the other.

Now the materialist would, of course, like to maintain that psychological states, such as feeling, believing, desiring, and so on, are really nothing but perfectly *familiar kinds* of material states, that is, states of the body, particularly of the brain and nervous system; states that are either observable or testable by the usual methods of biology, physics, and chemistry. But this, as we have seen earlier, seems to be a vain hope, and will always be an obstacle to any simple materialism. There is always, it seems, something that can be asserted of certain psychological states which makes little if any sense when asserted of any ordinary or familiar state of matter. One can say of a belief, for instance, that it is true or false, but this can never be said, except metaphorically or derivatively, of any familiar state of matter, such as an arrangement of molecules; we could say of such a thing that it is true or false, only if we first assumed that it is identical with some belief that is such. Again, one can say of a desire that it is the desire *for* this or that —for instance, the desire for food; of a fear that it is a fear *of* something—for instance, a fear of heights; but of no familiar state of matter can it be said that it is, in the same sense, *for* or *of* anything. It just *is* the state of matter that it is. Suppose, for example, that the materialist should say that the feeling of hunger is simply *identical* with a certain familiar state of the body; not merely that it is prompted by that state but that it *is* that state, and is describable in terms of the concepts of physics and chemistry. Thus, let us suppose him to claim that hunger just *is* the state consisting of having an empty stomach, together with a deficiency of certain salts or other substances in the blood, and a certain physical disequilibrium of the nervous system consequent upon these conditions. Now there is, of course, no doubt an intimate connection between such states as these and the desire for food, but the assertion of their *identity* with that desire will always be plagued because, unlike the desire, those bodily states can be fully described without mentioning food at all, and without saying that they are in any sense states that are *for* food. Indeed, the notion of something being *for* or *of* something else, in the sense in which a desire may be a desire *for* food, or a fear may be a fear *of* heights, is not a concept of physics or chemistry at all. And yet it can surely be said of a certain desire that it is a desire for food, or of a certain fear that it is a fear of heights. The referential character of such states seems, indeed, essential to any proper description of them. Significantly, when those substances that are physiologically associated with such states are artificially administered to someone, in the effort to create within him those states themselves, the effort fails. It is fairly well known, for example, what physiological changes a man undergoes when he is in a state of fear; but when these changes are artificially evoked in him, he does not experience fear in the usual sense. He describes his state as being vaguely *like* fear, but finds that he is not afraid *of* anything.

But while psychological states are thus evidently not identical with any familiar bodily states, it does not follow that they are identical with no state of matter at all. They may, in fact, be unfamiliar states of matter, that is, states of the body that are not observable or testable by the ordinary methods of biology, physics, and chemistry. This suggestion is not as question-begging as it appears, for it is conceded by the most resolute soul philosophers and dualists that psychological states are strange ones in this respect at least, that they are not thus observable. From the fact that some state is unobservable by the usual methods of scientific observation, nothing whatever follows with respect to the truth or falsity of materialism. From the fact that a certain state is in some respect unusual it does not follow that it is a state of an unusual thing, of a soul rather than a body, but rather, that if it is a state of the body it is an unusual one, and if it is a state of the soul it is no less unusual. Nothing is made clearer, more comprehensible, or less strange by postulating some new substance as the subject of certain states not familiar to the natural sciences, and then baptizing that new substance "the mind" or "the soul." Nor does one avoid materialism at this point by saying that by the "mind" or "soul" we just *mean* that which is the subject of psychological states; for while that might indeed be true, it is nevertheless an open question whether what we thus mean by the "mind" or "soul" might not turn out, after all, to be what we ordinarily denominate "the body." The existence of nothing whatever can be derived from any definitions of terms.

The soul   This point can perhaps be borne home to the imagination by the following sort of consideration. Suppose one feels, as probably everyone more or less does, that a *person* cannot be a mere *body*, and that no increase in the physical, biological, and physiological complexity of any body can bridge the gulf between being a body, albeit a complicated and living one, and being a person. Consider, then, a highly complex and living animal organism, physically and biologically identical in every respect to a living man, but lacking that one thing that is, we are supposing, still needed in order to convert this body into a person. Now just what can this extra essential ingredient be? What do we need to *add* to convert a mere body into a person?

Let us suppose it is a *soul.* If we add a soul to this living, complicated animal organism, let us suppose, then, *lo!* it will cease to be a mere body and become a person. No one knows, however, exactly what a soul is or what properties it must possess in order to confer personality upon something. All we can say is that it is what distinguishes a person from a mere body, which of course tells us nothing here. So let us give it some definite properties. It does not matter what properties we give it, as we shall shortly see, so to make it simple and easy to grasp, let us suppose that this soul is a small round ball, about the size of a marble, transparent and indestructible. Now clearly, by implanting *that* anywhere in the living organism we get no closer to converting it from a mere body to a person. We manage only to add one further, trivial complication. But why so? Why are we now no closer to having a person than before? Is it just because the "soul" we added is itself a mere body? If that is the difficulty, then let us remove its corporeality. Let us suppose that the soul we add to this living animal organism is not a small round *physical* ball but a nonphysical one. This will permit us to retain its transparency. If, being nonphysical, it can no longer be described as a ball, then we can drop that part of the description too. Let the thing we add be, in short, anything one likes. Let it be a small hard ball, a small soft ball, an immaterial ball, or something that is neither material nor a ball. The point is, that no matter *what* it is that is added, it goes not the least way toward converting what was a mere body into a person. If a small hard ball does not bridge the gap, then we get no closer to bridging it by simply removing its properties of hardness, smallness, and sphericity—by making it, in short, something that is merely *non*physical. What we need to do is state just what positive properties this extra thing must possess, in order to elevate an animal body to the status of a person, and no positive properties suggest themselves at all. We cannot give it psychological properties—by saying, for example, that this soul thinks, desires, deliberates, wills, believes, repents, and so on; for if the thing we are adding has *those* properties, than it is *already* a person in its own right, and there is no question of *adding* it to something in order to *get* a person. We could have as easily given *those* properties to the animal organism with which we began, as to give them to something else and then superfluously amalgamate the two things. Plainly, there are no positive properties of any soul that will do the trick. The best we can do is to say that the extra something required—the soul, or the mind, or whatever we choose to call this additional thing—is that which, when added, makes up the difference between being a mere animal body and being a person. This is about as good a way as one could find for indicating that he has no idea what he is talking about.

The "privacy"
of psychological
states

One final point will serve to illustrate the futility of dualistic hypotheses as solutions to difficulties admittedly inherent in any materialistic theory.

The states of the mind or soul, it is said, are simply those states that are not observable by any ordinary way but which can nevertheless be known, by an immediate awareness, to the person who has them. It is thus the *privacy* of such states that marks them as mental and, being mental, it is forthwith concluded that they are states of a mind or soul rather than of a body, and sometimes that the person who is aware of them is identical with that mind or soul. But concerning some such states—namely, pains and other simple sensations, which are most assuredly private—there is an absurdity in asserting that they are states of the mind or soul.

Suppose, for instance, that one has a decayed tooth, or a lacerated toe. Now the dentist, it is said, can observe, perhaps in minute detail, the condition of the tooth, and the physician the condition of the toe, but neither can have any awareness of the pain associated with either, pains that are nevertheless felt by him whose tooth or toe is thus damaged. The conclusion is then drawn that the dentist and physician are aware only of states of the body, while the patient is aware of something else which, being no state of the body, must be a state of the mind or soul.

But surely all that follows from such an argument is that persons other than oneself can observe some, but not others, of one's states. It does not at all follow that those private states—pains, in this case—are states of some further thing, such as a mind or soul, that is unobservable. From the fact that some state is, in the sense described, private, it does not follow that it is a state of a private thing. The argument is, in short, a simple *non sequitur*.

The conclusion of the argument is moreover absurd; for that conclusion is that a toothache or a toe ache is a state of mind, or a condition of the soul, which they manifestly are not. A toothache is a state of the tooth, and a toe ache a state of the toe. That the dentist and physician cannot observe these states does not show that they are states of the mind or soul rather than of the tooth and toe, but only that some of a man's states are not observable to dentists and doctors, which is hardly surprising. The physician, contemplating one's lacerated toe, might reasonably ask whether *it* hurts, and in doing so he would be inquiring about the toe and nothing else. The pain that the patient feels, moreover, is felt in the toe. It would be an utter distortion to say that the pain is felt in, or by, the mind, and then somehow *referred* to the toe. And it would be not only a distortion, but an absurdity, for the patient to say that he feels pain in his mind, or that a pain is felt by his mind, this pain being occasioned by a condition of his toe. The pain is located, by the patient, in his toe, just as surely as the wound; that is where the pain is felt, nowhere else. What the patient can truly say is that *he* feels pain and that the pain he feels is in his toe. In thus referring to himself as the subject of the feeling, he is not referring to some metaphysical thing, like a soul or mind, and saying that *it* feels pain; he is referring to himself, as a man—that is, as a living, animal organism, seated here and now before the physician, an animal organism with which he identifies himself, and saying that this man, himself, feels pain. And the pain that he feels, he surely does not doubt, is in his toe. At no point in his discussion with the physician could it ever be relevant in this situation to make any reference to his mind or his soul; it is not the soul or mind that hurts but the toe, nor is it the soul or mind that feels it, but he himself, the very man, the very animal organism, the very living, physical body that is sitting there.

Of course we cannot, by these reflections, pretend to have solved the problems of mind and matter, nor to have proved any theory of materialism. Human nature is mysterious, and remains so, no matter what one's metaphysical theory is or how simple it is. It does nevertheless seem evident that no dualistic theory of man renders human nature any less mysterious, and that whatever questions are left unanswered by the materialist are left equally unanswered, though perhaps better concealed, by his opponents.

FREEDOM

AND DETERMINISM

4

If I consider the world or any part of it at any particular moment, it seems certain that it is perfectly determinate in every detail. There is no vagueness, looseness, or ambiguity. There is, indeed, vagueness, and even error, in my conceptions of reality, but not in reality itself. A lilac bush, which surely has a certain exact number of blossoms, appears to me only to have many blossoms, and I do not know how many. Things seen in the distance appear of indefinite form, and often of a color and size which in fact they have not. Things near the border of my visual field seem to me vague and amorphous, and I can never even say exactly where that border itself is, it is so indefinite and vague. But all such indeterminateness resides solely in my conceptions and ideas; the world itself shares none of it. The sea, at any exact time and place, has exactly a certain salinity and temperature, and every grain of sand on its shore is exactly disposed with respect to all the others. The wind at any point in space has at any moment a certain direction and force, not more nor less. It matters not whether these properties and relations are known to anyone. A field of wheat at any moment contains just an exact number of ripening grains, each having reached just the ripeness it exhibits, each presenting a determinate color and shade, an exact shape and mass. A man, too, at any given point in his life, is perfectly determinate to the minutest cells of his body. My own brain, nerves—even my thoughts, intentions and feelings—are at any moment just what they then specifically are. These thoughts might, to be sure, be vague and even false as representations, but as thoughts they are not, and even a false idea is no less an exact and determinate idea than a true one.

Nothing seems more obvious. But if I now ask *why* the world and all its larger or smaller parts are this moment just what they are, the answer comes to mind: Because the world, the moment before, was precisely what it then was. Given exactly what went before, the world, it seems, could now be none other than it is. And what it was a moment before, in all its larger and minuter parts, was the consequence of what had gone just before then, and so on, back to the very beginning of the world, if it had a beginning, or through an infinite past time, in case it had not. In any case, the world as it now is, and every part of it, and every detail of every part, would seem to be the only world that now could be, given just what it has been.

Determinism   Reflections such as these suggest that, in the case of everything that exists, there are antecedent conditions, known or unknown, given which that thing could not be other than it is. This is an exact statement of the metaphysical thesis of determinism. More loosely, it says that everything, including every cause, is the effect of some cause or causes; or that everything is not only determinate but causally determined. The statement, moreover, makes no allowance for time, for past, or for future. Hence, if true, it holds not only for all things that have existed but for all things that do or ever will exist.

Of course men rarely think of such a principle, and hardly one in a thousand will ever formulate it to himself in words. Yet all men do seem to assume it in their daily affairs, so much so that some philosophers have declared it an a priori principle of the understanding, that is, something that is known independently of experience, while others have deemed it to be at least a part of the common sense of mankind. Thus, when I hear a noise I look up to see where it came from. I never suppose that it was just a noise that came from nowhere and had no cause. All men do the same—even animals, though they have never once thought about metaphysics or the principle of universal determinism. Men believe, or at least act as though they believed, that things have causes, without exception. When a child or animal touches a hot stove for the first time, it unhesitatingly believes that the pain then felt was caused by that stove, and so firm and immediate is that belief that hot stoves are avoided ever after. We all use our metaphysical principles, whether we think of them or not, or are even capable of thinking of them. If I have a bodily or other disorder—a rash, for instance, or a fever or a phobia—I consult a physician for a diagnosis and explanation, in the hope that the cause of it might be found and removed or moderated. I am never tempted to suppose that such things just have no causes, arising from nowhere, else I would take no steps to remove the causes. The principle of determinism is here, as in everything else, simply assumed, without being thought about.

Determinism and human behavior

I am a part of the world. So is each of the cells and minute parts of which I am composed. The principle of determinism, then, in case it is true, applies to me and to each of those minute parts, no less than to the sand, wheat, winds, and waters of which we have spoken. There is no particular difficulty in thinking so, as long as I consider only what are sometimes called the "purely physiological" changes of my body, like growth, the pulse, glandular secretions, and the like. But what of my thoughts and ideals? And what of my behavior that is supposed to be deliberate, purposeful, and perhaps morally significant? These are all changes of my own being, changes that I undergo, and if these are all but the consequences of the conditions under which they occur, and these conditions are the only ones that could have obtained, given the state of the world just before and when they arose, what now becomes of my responsibility for my behavior and of the control over my conduct that I fancy myself to possess? What am I but a helpless product of nature, destined by her to do whatever I do and to become whatever I become?

There is no moral blame nor merit in any man who cannot help what he does. It matters not whether the explanation for his behavior is found within him or without, whether it is expressed in terms of ordinary physical causes or allegedly "mental" ones, or whether the causes be proximate or remote. I am not responsible for being a man rather than a woman, nor for having the temperament, desires, purposes, and ideals characteristic of that sex. I was never asked whether these should be given to me. The kleptomaniac, similarly, steals from compulsion, the chronic alcoholic drinks from compulsion, and sometimes even the hero dies from compulsive courage. Though these causes are within them, they compel no less for that, and their victims never chose to have them inflicted upon themselves. To say they are compulsions is to say only that they compel. But to say they compel is only to say that they cause; for the cause of a thing being given, the effect cannot fail to follow. By the thesis of determinism, however, everything whatever is caused, and not one single thing could ever be other than exactly what it is. Perhaps one thinks that the kleptomaniac and the drunkard did not have to become what they are, that they could have done better at another time and thereby ended up better than they are now, or that the hero could have done worse and then ended up a coward. But this shows only an unwillingness to understand what made them become as they are. Having found that their behavior is caused from within them, we can hardly avoid asking what caused these inner springs of action, and then asking what were the causes of these causes, and so on through the infinite past. We shall not, certainly, with our small understanding and our fragmentary knowledge of the past ever know why the world should at just this time and place have produced just this thief, this drunkard, and this hero, but the vagueness and smatteringness of our knowledge should not tempt us to imagine a similar vagueness in nature herself. Everything in nature is and always has been determinate, with no loose edges at all, and she was forever destined to bring forth just what she has produced, however slight may be our understanding of the origins of these works. Ultimate responsibility for anything that exists, and hence for any man and his deeds, can thus only rest with the first cause of all things, if there is such a cause, or nowhere at all, in case there is not. Such at least seems to be the unavoidable implication of determinism.

Determinism and morals

Some philosophers, faced with all this, which seems quite clear to the ordinary understanding, have tried to cling to determinism while modifying traditional conceptions of morals. They continue to *use* such words as "merit," "blame," "praise," and "desert," but they so divest them of their meanings as to finish by talking about things entirely different, sometimes without themselves realizing that they are no longer on the subject. An ordinary man will hardly understand that anyone can possess merit or vice and be deserving of moral praise or blame, as a result of traits that he has or of behavior arising from those traits, once it is well understood that he could never have avoided being just what he is and doing just what he does.

We are happily spared going into all this, however, for the question whether determinism is true of human nature is not a question of ethics at all but of metaphysics. There is accordingly no hope of answering it within the context of ethics. One can, to be sure, simply *assume* an answer to it—assume that determinism is true, for instance—and then see what are the implications of this answer for ethics; but that does not answer the question. Or one can *assume* some theory or other of ethics—assume some version of "the greatest happiness" principle, for instance—and then see whether that theory is consistent with determinism. But such confrontations of theories with theories likewise makes us no wiser, so far as any fundamental question is concerned. We can suppose at once that determinism is consistent with some conceptions of morals, and inconsistent with others, and that the same holds for indeterminism. We shall still not know what theories are true; we shall only know which are consistent with each other.

We shall, then, eschew all considerations of ethics, as having no real bearing on our problem. We want to learn, if we can, whether determinism is true, and this is a question of metaphysics. It can, like all good questions of philosophy, be answered only on the basis of certain data; that is, by seeing whether or not it squares with certain things which every man knows, or believes himself to know, or things of which every man is at least more sure than the answer to the question at issue.

Now I could, of course, simply affirm that I am a morally responsible being, in the sense in which my responsibility for my behavior implies that I could have avoided that behavior. But this would take us into the nebulous realm of ethics, and it is, in fact, far from obvious that I am responsible in that sense. Many have doubted that they are responsible in that sense, and it is in any case not difficult to doubt it, however strongly one might feel about it.

There are, however, two things about myself of which I feel quite certain and which have no necessary connection with morals. The first is that I sometimes deliberate, with the view to making a decision; a decision, namely, to do this thing or that. And the second is that whether or not I deliberate about what to do, it is sometimes up to me what I do. This might all be an illusion, of course; but so also any philosophical theory, such as the theory of determinism, might be false. The point remains that it is far more difficult for me to doubt that I sometimes deliberate, and that it is sometimes up to me what to do, than to doubt any philosophical theory whatever, including the theory of determinism. We must, accordingly, if we ever hope to be wiser, adjust our theories to our data and not try to adjust our data to our theories.

Let us, then, get these two data quite clearly before us so we can see what they are, what they presuppose, and what they do and do not entail.

Deliberation   Deliberation is an activity, or at least a kind of experience, that cannot be defined, or even described without metaphors. We speak of weighing this and that in our minds, of trying to anticipate consequences of various possible courses of action, and so on, but such descriptions do not convey to us what deliberation is unless we already know.

Whenever I deliberate, however, I find that I make certain presuppositions, whether I actually think of them or not. That is, I assume that certain things are true, certain things which are such that, if I thought they were not true, it would be impossible for me to deliberate at all. Some of these can be listed as follows.

First, I find that I can deliberate only about my own behavior and never about the behavior of another. I can try to guess, speculate, or figure out what another person is going to do; I can read certain signs and sometimes infer what he will do; but I cannot deliberate about it. When I deliberate I try to decide something, to make up my mind, and this is as remote as anything could be from speculating, trying to guess, or to infer from signs. Sometimes one *does* speculate on what he is going to do, by trying to draw conclusions from certain signs or omens—he might infer that he is going to sneeze, for instance, or speculate that he is going to become a grandfather—but he is not then deliberating whether to do these things or not. One does, to be sure, sometimes deliberate about whether another person will do a certain act, when that other person is subject to his command or otherwise under his control; but then he is not really deliberating about another person's acts at all, but about his own—namely, whether or not to have that other person carry out the order.

Second, I find that I can deliberate only about future things, never things past or present. I may not know what I did at a certain time in the past, in case I have forgotten, but I can no longer deliberate whether to do it then or not. I can, again, only speculate, guess, try to infer, or perhaps try to remember. Similarly, I cannot deliberate whether or not to be doing something now; I can only ascertain whether or not I am in fact doing it. If I am sitting I cannot deliberate about whether or not to be sitting. I can only deliberate about whether to remain sitting—and this has to do with the future.

Third, I cannot deliberate about what I shall do, in case I already know what I am going to do. If I were to say, for example, "I know that I am going to be married tomorrow and in the meantime I am going to deliberate about whether to get married," I would contradict myself. There are only two ways that I could know now what I am going to do tomorrow; namely, either by inferring this from certain signs and omens or by having already decided what I am going to do. But if I have inferred from signs and omens what I am going to do, I cannot deliberate about it—there is just nothing for me to decide; and similarly, if I have already decided. If, on the other hand, I can still deliberate about what I am going to do, to that extent I must regard the signs and omens as unreliable, and the inference uncertain, and I do not therefore know what I am going to do after all.

And finally, I cannot deliberate about what to do, even though I may not know what I am going to do, unless I believe that it is up to me what I am going to do. If I am within the power of another person, or at the mercy of circumstances over which I have no control, then, although I may have no idea what I am going to do, I cannot deliberate about it. I can only wait and see. If, for instance, I am a conscript, and regulations regarding uniforms are posted each day by my commanding officer and are strictly enforced by him, then I shall not know what uniforms I shall be wearing from time to time, but I cannot deliberate about it. I can only wait and see what regulations are posted; it is not up to me. Similarly, a woman who is about to give birth to a child cannot deliberate whether to have a boy or a girl, even though she may not know. She can only wait and see; it is not up to her. Such examples can be generalized to cover any case wherein one does not know what he is going to do, but believes that it is not up to him, and hence no matter for his decision and hence none for his deliberation.

"It is up to me"   I sometimes feel certain that it is, at least to some extent, up to me what I am going to do; indeed, I must believe this if I am to deliberate about what to do. But what does this mean? It is, again, hard to say, but the idea can be illustrated, and we can fairly easily see what it does not mean.

Let us consider the simplest possible sort of situation in which this belief might be involved. At this moment, for instance, it seems quite certain to me that, holding my finger before me, I can move it either to the left or to the right, that each of these motions is possible for me. This does not mean merely that my finger can move either way, although it entails that, for this would be true in case nothing obstructed it, even if I had no control over it at all. I can say of a distant, fluttering leaf that it can move either way, but not that I can move it, since I have no control over it. How it moves is not up to me. Nor does it mean merely that my finger can be moved either way, although it entails this too. If the motions of my finger are under the control of some other person or of some machine, then it might be true that the finger can be moved either way, by that person or machine, though false that I can move it at all.

If I say, then, that it is up to me how I move my finger, I mean that I can move it in this way and I can move it in that way, and not merely that it can move or be moved in this way and that. I mean that the motion of my finger is within my direct control. If someone were to ask me to move it to the right, I could do that, and if he were to ask me to move it to the left, I could do that too. Further, I could do these simple acts without being asked at all, and, having been asked, I could move it in a manner the exact opposite of what was requested, since I can ignore the request. There are, to be sure, some motions of my finger that I cannot make, so it is not *entirely* up to me how it moves. I cannot bend it backward, for instance, or bend it into a knot, for these motions are obstructed by the very anatomical construction of the finger itself; and to say that I can move my finger at all means at least that nothing obstructs such a motion, though it does not mean merely this. There is, however, at this moment, no obstruction, anatomical or otherwise, to my moving it to the right, and none to my moving it to the left.

This datum, it should be noted, is properly expressed as a conjunction and not as a disjunction. That is, my belief is that I can move my finger in one way, *and* that I can also move it another way; and it does not do justice to this belief to say that I can move it one way *or* the other. It is fairly easy to see the truth of this, for the latter claim, that I can move it one way *or* the other, would be satisfied in case there were only one way I could move it, and *that* is not what I believe. Suppose, for instance, my hand were strapped to a device in such a fashion that I could move my finger to the right but not to the left. Then it would still be entirely true that I could move it either to the left *or* to the right—since it would be true that I could move it to the right. But that is not what I now believe. My finger is not strapped to anything, and nothing obstructs its motion in either direction. And what I believe, in this situation, is that I can move it to the right *and* I can move it to the left.

We must note further that the belief expressed in our datum is not a belief in what is logically impossible. It is the belief that I now *can* move my finger in different ways but not that I can move it in different ways at once. What I believe is that I am now able to move my finger one way and that I am now equally able to move it another way, but I do not claim to be able now or any other time to move it both ways simultaneously. The situation here is analogous to one in which I might, for instance, be offered a choice of either of two apples but forbidden to take both. Each apple is such that I may select it, but neither is such that I may select it together with the other.

Now are these two data—the belief that I do sometimes deliberate, and the belief that it is sometimes up to me what I do— consistent with the metaphysical theory of determinism? We do not know yet. We intend to find out. It is fairly clear, however, that they are going to present difficulties to that theory. But let us not, in any case, try to avoid those difficulties by just denying the data themselves. If we eventually deny the data, we shall do so for better reasons than this. Virtually all men are convinced that beliefs such as are expressed in our data are sometimes true. They cannot be simply dismissed as false just because they might appear to conflict with a metaphysical theory that hardly any men have ever really thought much about at all. Almost any man, unless his fingers are paralyzed, bound, or otherwise incapable of movement, believes sometimes that the motions of his fingers are within his control, in exactly the sense expressed by our data. If consequences of considerable importance to him depend on how he moves his fingers, he sometimes deliberates before moving them, or at least, he is convinced that he does, or that he can. Philosophers might have different notions of just what things are implied by such data, but there is in any case no more, and in fact considerably less, reason for denying the data than for denying some philosophical theory.

Causal vs. logical necessity
Philosophers have long since pointed out that causal connections involve no logical necessity, that the denial of a particular causal connection is never self-contradictory, and this is undoubtedly true. But neither does the assertion or the denial of determinism involve any concept of what is and what is not logically necessary. If determinism is true, then anything that happens is, given the conditions under which it occurs, the only thing possible, the thing that is necessitated by those conditions. But it is not the only thing that is logically possible, nor do those conditions logically necessitate it. Similarly, if one denies the thesis of determinism, by asserting, for instance, that each of two bodily motions is possible for him under identical conditions, he is asserting much more than that each is logically possible, for that would be a trivial claim.

This distinction, between logical necessity and the sort of necessity involved in determinism, can be illustrated with examples. If, for instance, a man is beheaded, we can surely say that it is impossible for him to go on living, that his being beheaded necessitates his death, and so on; but there are no logical necessities or impossibilities involved here. It is not logically impossible for a man to live without his head. Yet no one will deny that a man cannot live under conditions that include his being headless, that such a state of affairs is in a perfectly clear sense impossible. Similarly, if my finger is in a tight and fairly strong cast, then it is impossible for me to move it in any way at all, though this is not logically impossible. It is logically possible that I should be vastly stronger than I am, and that I should move it and, in doing so, break the cast, though this would ordinarily not be possible in the sense that concerns us. Again, it is not logically impossible that I should bend my finger backward, or into a knot, though it is, in fact, impossible for me to do either or, what means the same thing, necessary that I should do neither. Certain conditions prohibit my doing such things, though they impose no logical barrier. And finally, if someone—a physician, for example—should ask me whether I can move my finger, and I should reply truly that I can, I would not merely be telling him that it is logically possible for me to move it, for this he already knows. I would be telling him that I am able to move it, that it is within my power to do so, that there are no conditions, such as paralysis or whatnot, that prevent my moving it.

It follows that not all necessity is logical necessity, nor all impossibility logical impossibility, and that to say that something is possible is sometimes to say much more than that it is logically possible. The kind of necessity involved in the thesis of determinism is quite obviously the nonlogical kind, as is also the kind of possibility involved in its denial. If we needed a *name* for these nonlogical modalities, we could call them *causal* necessity, impossibility, and possibility, but the concepts are clear enough without making a great deal of the name.

Freedom   To say that it is, in a given instance, up to me what I do, is to say that I am in that instance *free* with respect to what I then do. Thus, I am sometimes free to move my finger this way and that, but not, certainly, to bend it backward or into a knot. But what does this mean?

It means, first, that there is no *obstacle* or *impediment* to my activity. Thus, there is sometimes no obstacle to my moving my finger this way and that, though there are obvious obstacles to my moving it far backward or into a knot. Those things, accordingly, that pose obstacles to my motions limit my freedom. If my hand were strapped in such a way as to permit only a leftward motion of my finger, I would not then be free to move it to the right. If it were encased in a tight cast that permitted no motion, I would not be free to move it at all. Freedom of motion, then, is limited by obstacles.

Further, to say that it is, in a given instance, up to me what I do, means that nothing *constrains* or *forces* me to do one thing rather than another. Constraints are like obstacles, except that while the latter prevent, the former enforce. Thus, if my finger is being forcibly bent to the left—by a machine, for instance, or by another person, or by any force that I cannot overcome—then I am not free to move it this way and that. I cannot, in fact, move it at all; I can only watch to see how it is moved, and perhaps vainly resist. Its motions are not up to me, or within my control, but in the control of some other thing or person.

Obstacles and constraints, then, both obviously limit my freedom. To say I am free to perform some action thus means at least that there is no obstacle to my doing it, and that nothing constrains me to do otherwise.

Now if we rest content with this observation, as many have, and construe free activity simply as activity that is unimpeded and unconstrained, there is evidently no inconsistency between affirming both the thesis of determinism and the claim that I am sometimes free. For to say that some action of mine is neither impeded nor constrained does not by itself imply that it is not causally determined. The absence of obstacles and constraints are mere negative conditions, and do not by themselves rule out the presence of positive causes. It might seem, then, that we can say of some of my actions that there are conditions antecedent to their performance so that no other actions were possible, and also that these actions were unobstructed and unconstrained. And to say that would logically entail that such actions were both causally determined, and free.

Soft determinism   It is this kind of consideration that has led many philosophers to embrace what is sometimes called "soft determinism." All versions of this theory have in common three claims, by means of which, it is naïvely supposed, a reconciliation is achieved between determinism and freedom. Freedom being, furthermore, a condition of moral responsibility and the only condition that metaphysics seriously questions, it is supposed by the partisans of this view that determinism is perfectly compatible with such responsibility. This, no doubt, accounts for its great appeal and wide acceptance, even by some men of considerable learning.

The three claims of soft determinism are (1) that the thesis of determinism is true, and that accordingly all human behavior, voluntary or other, like the behavior of all other things, arises from antecedent conditions, given which no other behavior is possible—in short, that all human behavior is caused and determined; (2) that voluntary behavior is nonetheless free to the extent that it is not externally constrained or impeded; and (3) that, in the absence of such obstacles and constraints, the causes of voluntary behavior are certain states, events, or conditions within the agent himself; namely, his own acts of will or volitions, choices, decisions, desires, and so on.

Thus, on this view, I am free, and therefore sometimes responsible for what I do, provided nothing prevents me from acting according to my own choice, desire or volition, or constrains me to act otherwise. There may, to be sure, be other conditions for my responsibility—such as, for example, an understanding of the probable consequences of my behavior, and that sort of thing—but absence of constraint or impediment is, at least, one such condition. And, it is claimed, it is a condition that is compatible with the supposition that my behavior is caused—for it is, by hypothesis, caused by my own inner choices, desires, and volitions.

The theory of soft determinism looks good at first—so good that it has for generations been solemnly taught from numberless philosophical chairs and implanted in the minds of students as sound philosophy—but no great acumen is needed to discover that far from solving any problem, it only camouflages it.

My free actions are those unimpeded and unconstrained motions that arise from my own inner desires, choices, and volitions; let us grant this provisionally. But now, whence arise those inner states that determine what my body shall do? Are they within my control or not? Having made my choice or decision and acted upon it, could I have chosen otherwise or not?

Here the determinist, hoping to surrender nothing and yet to avoid the problem implied in that question, bids us not to ask it; the question itself, he announces, is without meaning. For to say that I could have done otherwise, he says, means only that I *would* have done otherwise *if* those inner states that determined my action had been different; if, that is, I had decided or chosen differently. To ask, accordingly, whether I could have chosen or decided differently is only to ask whether, had I decided to decide differently or chosen to choose differently, or willed to will differently, I would have decided or chosen or willed differently. And this, of course, *is* unintelligible nonsense.

But it is not nonsense to ask whether the causes of my actions—my own inner choices, decisions and desires—are themselves caused. And of course they are, if determinism is true, for on that thesis everything is caused and determined. And if they are, then we cannot avoid concluding that, given the causal conditions of those inner states, I could not have decided, willed, chosen, or desired otherwise than I in fact did, for this is a logical consequence of the very definition of determinism. Of course we can still say that, *if* the causes of those inner states, whatever they were, had been different, then their effects, those inner states themselves, would have been different, and that in this hypothetical sense I could have decided, chosen, willed, or desired differently—but that only pushes our problem back still another step. For we will then want to know whether the causes of those inner states were within my control; and so on, *ad infinitum*. We are, at each step, permitted to say "could have been otherwise" only in a provisional sense—provided, that is, something else had been different—but must then retract it and replace it with "could not have been otherwise" as soon as we discover, as we must at each step, that whatever would have to have been different could not have been different.

Examples   Such is the dialectic of the problem. The easiest way to see the shadowy quality of soft determinism, however, is by means of examples.

Let us suppose that my body is moving in various ways, that these motions are not externally constrained or impeded, and that they are all exactly in accordance with my own desires, choices, or acts of will and what not. When I will that my arm should move in a certain way, I find it moving in that way, unobstructed and unconstrained. When I will to speak, my lips and tongue move, unobstructed and unconstrained, in a manner suitable to the formation of the words I choose to utter. Now given that this is a correct description of my behavior, namely, that it consists of the unconstrained and unimpeded motions of my body in response to my own volitions, then it follows that my behavior is free, on the soft determinist's definition of "free." It follows further that I am responsible for that behavior; or at least, that if I am not, it is not from any lack of freedom on my part.

But if the fulfillment of these conditions renders my behavior free—that is to say, if my behavior satisfies the conditions of free action set forth in the theory of soft determinism—then my behavior will be no less free if we assume further conditions that are perfectly consistent with those already satisfied.

We suppose further, accordingly, that while my behavior is entirely in accordance with my own volitions, and thus "free" in terms of the conception of freedom we are examining, my volitions themselves are caused. To make this graphic, we can suppose that an ingenious physiologist can induce in me any volition he pleases, simply by pushing various buttons on an instrument to which, let us suppose, I am attached by numerous wires. All the volitions I have in that situation are, accordingly, precisely the ones he gives me. By pushing one button, he evokes in me the volition to raise my hand; and my hand, being unimpeded, rises in response to that volition. By pushing another, he induces the volition in me to kick, and my foot, being unimpeded, kicks in response to that volition. We can even suppose that the physiologist puts a rifle in my hands, aims it at some passer-by, and then, by pushing the proper button, evokes in me the volition to squeeze my finger against the trigger, whereupon the passer-by falls dead of a bullet wound.

This is the description of a man who is acting in accordance with his inner volitions, a man whose body is unimpeded and unconstrained in its motions, these motions being the effects of those inner states. It is hardly the description of a free and responsible agent. It is the perfect description of a puppet. To render a man your puppet, it is not necessary forcibly to constrain the motions of his limbs, after the fashion that real puppets are moved. A subtler but no less effective means of making a man your puppet would be to gain complete control of his inner states, and ensuring, as the theory of soft determinism does ensure, that his body will move in accordance with them.

The example is somewhat unusual, but it is no worse for that. It is perfectly intelligible, and it does appear to refute the soft determinist's conception of freedom. One might think that, in such a case, the agent should not have allowed himself to be so rigged in the first place, but this is irrelevant; we can suppose that he was not aware that he was, and was hence unaware of the source of those inner states that prompted his bodily motions. The example can, moreover, be modified in perfectly realistic ways, so as to coincide with actual and familiar cases. One can, for instance, be given a compulsive desire for certain drugs, simply by having them administered to him over a course of time. Suppose, then, that I do, with neither my knowledge nor consent, thus become a victim of such a desire and act upon it. Do I act freely, merely by virtue of the fact that I am unimpeded in my quest for drugs? In a sense I do, surely, but I am hardly free with respect to whether or not I shall use drugs. I never chose to have the desire for them inflicted upon me.

Nor does it, of course, matter whether the inner states which allegedly prompt all my "free" activity are evoked in me by another agent or by perfectly impersonal forces. Whether a desire which causes my body to behave in a certain way is inflicted upon me by another person, for instance, or derived from hereditary factors, or indeed from anything at all, matters not the least. In any case, if it is in fact the cause of my bodily behavior, I cannot but act in accordance with it. Wherever it came from, whether from personal or impersonal origins, it was entirely caused or determined, and not within my control. Indeed, if determinism is true, as the theory of soft determinism holds it to be, all those inner states which cause my body to behave in whatever ways it behaves must arise from circumstances that existed before I was born; for the chain of causes and effects is infinite, and none could have been the least different, given those that preceded.

Simple indeterminism

We might at first now seem warranted in simply denying determinism, and saying that, insofar as they are free, my actions are not caused; or that, if they are caused by my own inner states—my own desires, impulses, choices, volitions, and whatnot—then these, in any case, are not caused. This is a perfectly clear sense in which a man's action, assuming that it was free, could have been otherwise. If it was uncaused, then, even given the conditions under which it occurred and all that preceded, some other act was nonetheless possible, and he did not have to do what he did. Or if his action was the inevitable consequence of his own inner states, and could not have been otherwise given these, we can nevertheless say that these inner states, being uncaused, could have been otherwise, and could thereby have produced different actions.

Only the slightest consideration will show, however, that this simple denial of determinism has not the slightest plausibility. For let us suppose it is true, and that some of my bodily motions—namely, those that I regard as my free acts—are not caused at all or, if caused by my own inner states, that these are not caused. We shall thereby avoid picturing a puppet, to be sure—but only by substituting something even less like a man; for the conception that now emerges is not that of a free man, but of an erratic and jerking phantom, without any rhyme or reason at all.

Suppose that my right arm is free, according to this conception; that is, that its motions are uncaused. It moves this way and that from time to time, but nothing causes these motions. Sometimes it moves forth vigorously, sometimes up, sometimes down, sometimes it just drifts vaguely about—these motions all being wholly free and uncaused. Manifestly I have nothing to do with them at all; they just happen, and neither I nor anyone can ever tell what this arm will be doing next. It might seize a club and lay it on the head of the nearest bystander, no less to my astonishment than his. There will never be any point in asking why these motions occur, or in seeking any explanation of them, for under the conditions assumed there is no explanation. They just happen, from no causes at all.

This is no description of free, voluntary, or responsible behavior. Indeed, so far as the motions of my body or its parts are entirely uncaused, such motions cannot even be ascribed to me as my behavior in the first place, since I have nothing to do with them. The behavior of my arm is just the random motion of a foreign object. Behavior that is mine must be behavior that is within my control, but motions that occur from no causes are without the control of anyone. I can have no more to do with, and no more control over, the uncaused motions of my limbs than a gambler has over the motions of an honest roulette wheel. I can only, like him, idly wait to see what happens.

Nor does it improve things to suppose that my bodily motions are caused by my own inner states, so long as we suppose these to be wholly uncaused. The result will be the same as before. My arm, for example, will move this way and that, sometimes up and sometimes down, sometimes vigorously and sometimes just drifting about, always in response to certain inner states, to be sure. But since these are supposed to be wholly uncaused, it follows that I have no control over them and hence none over their effects. If my hand lays a club force-fully on the nearest bystander, we can indeed say that this motion resulted from an inner club-wielding desire of mine; but we must add that I had nothing to do with that desire, and that it arose, to be fol-lowed by its inevitable effect, no less to my astonishment than to his. Things like this do, alas, sometimes happen. We are all sometimes seized by compulsive impulses that arise we know not whither, and we do sometimes act upon these. But since they are far from being exam-ples of free, voluntary, and responsible behavior, we need only to learn that behavior was of this sort to conclude that it was not free, volun-tary, nor responsible. It was erratic, impulsive, and irresponsible.

Determinism and simple indeterminism as theories   Both determinism and simple indeterminism are loaded with diffi-culties, and no one who has thought much on them can affirm either of them without some embarrassment. Simple indetermin-ism has nothing whatever to be said for it, except that it appears to remove the grossest difficulties of determinism, only, however, to imply perfect absurdities of its own. Determinism, on the other hand, is at least initially plausible. Men seem to have a natural inclina-tion to believe in it; it is, indeed, almost required for the very exercise of practical intelligence. And beyond this, our experience appears always to confirm it, so long as we are dealing with everyday facts of common experience, as distinguished from the esoteric researches of theoretical physics. But determinism, as applied to human behavior, has implica-tions which few men can casually accept, and they appear to be im-plications which no modification of the theory can efface.

Both theories, moreover, appear logically irreconcilable to the two items of data that we set forth at the outset; namely, (1) that my be-havior is sometimes the outcome of my deliberation, and (2) that in these and other cases it is sometimes up to me what I do. Since these were our data, it is important to see, as must already be quite clear, that these theories cannot be reconciled to them.

I can deliberate only about my own future actions, and then only if I do not already know what I am going to do. If a certain nasal tickle warns me that I am about to sneeze, for instance, then I cannot de-liberate whether to sneeze or not; I can only prepare for the impending convulsion. But if determinism is true, then there are always conditions existing antecedently to everything I do, sufficient for my doing just that, and such as to render it inevitable. If I can know what those conditions are and what behavior they are sufficient to produce, then I can in every such case know what I am going to do and cannot then deliberate about it.

By itself this only shows, of course, that I can deliberate only in ignorance of the causal conditions of my behavior; it does not show that such conditions cannot exist. It is odd, however, to suppose that deliberation should be a mere substitute for clear knowledge. Ignorance is a condition of speculation, inference, and guesswork, which have nothing whatever to do with deliberation. A prisoner awaiting execution may not know when he is going to die, and he may even entertain the hope of reprieve, but he cannot deliberate about this. He can only speculate, guess—and wait.

Worse yet, however, it now becomes clear that I cannot deliberate about what I am going to do, if it is even possible for me to find out in advance, whether I do in fact find out in advance or not. I can deliberate only with the view to deciding what to do, to making up my mind; and this is impossible if I believe that it could be inferred what I am going to do, from conditions already existing, even though I have not made that inference myself. If I believe that what I am going to do has been rendered inevitable by conditions already existing, and could be inferred by anyone having the requisite sagacity, then I cannot try to decide whether to do it or not, for there is simply nothing left to decide. I can at best only guess or try to figure it out myself or, all prognostics failing, I can wait and see; but I cannot deliberate. I deliberate in order to *decide* what *to* do, not to *discover* what it is that I am *going* to do. But if determinism is true, then there are always antecedent conditions sufficient for everything that I do, and this can always be inferred by anyone having the requisite sagacity; that is, by anyone having a knowledge of what those conditions are and what behavior they are sufficient to produce.

This suggests what in fact seems quite clear, that determinism cannot be reconciled with our second datum either, to the effect that it is sometimes up to me what I am going to do. For if it is ever really up to me whether to do this thing or that, then, as we have seen, each alternative course of action must be such that I can do it; not that I can do it in some abstruse or hypothetical sense of "can"; not that I could do it if only something were true that is not true; but in the sense that it is then and there within my power to do it. But this is never so, if determinism is true, for on the very formulation of that theory whatever happens at any time is the only thing that can then happen, given all that precedes it. It is simply a logical consequence of this that whatever I do at any time is the only thing I can then do, given the conditions that precede my doing it. Nor does it help in the least to interpose, among the causal antecedents of my behavior, my own inner states, such as my desires, choices, acts of will, and so on. For even supposing these to be always involved in voluntary behavior—which is highly doubtful in itself—it is a consequence of determinism that these, whatever they are at any time, can never be other than what they then are. Every chain of causes and effects, if determinism is true, is infinite. This is why it is not now up to me whether I shall a moment hence be male or female. The conditions determining my sex have existed through my whole life, and even prior to my life. But if determinism is true, the same holds of anything that I ever am, ever become, or ever do. It matters not whether we are speaking of the most patent facts of my being, such as my sex; or the most subtle, such as my feelings, thoughts, desires, or choices. Nothing could be other than it is, given what was; and while we may indeed say, quite idly, that something— some inner state of mine, for instance—*could* have been different, had only something *else* been different, any consolation of this thought evaporates as soon as we add that whatever would have to have been different could not have been different.

It is even more obvious that our data cannot be reconciled to the theory of simple indeterminism. I can deliberate only about my own actions; this is obvious. But the random, uncaused motion of any body whatever, whether it be a part of my body or not, is no action of mine and nothing that is within my power. I might try to guess what these motions will be, just as I might try to guess how a roulette wheel will behave, but I cannot deliberate about them or try to decide what they shall be, simply because these things are not up to me. Whatever is not caused by anything is not caused by me, and nothing could be more plainly inconsistent with saying that it is nevertheless up to me what it shall be.

The theory of agency   The only conception of action that accords with our data is one according to which men—and perhaps some other things too—are sometimes, but of course not always, self-determining beings; that is, beings which are sometimes the causes of their own behavior. In the case of an action that is free, it must be such that it is caused by the agent who performs it, but such that no antecedent conditions were sufficient for his performing just that action. In the case of an action that is both free and rational, it must be such that the agent who performed it did so for some reason, but this reason cannot have been the cause of it.

Now this conception fits what men take themselves to be; namely, beings who act, or who are agents, rather than things that are merely acted upon, and whose behavior is simply the causal consequence of conditions which they have not wrought. When I believe that I have done something, I do believe that it was I who caused it to be done, I who made something happen, and not merely something within me, such as one of my own subjective states, which is not identical with myself. If I believe that something not identical with myself was the cause of my behavior—some event wholly external to myself, for instance, or even one internal to myself, such as a nerve impulse, volition, or what not—then I cannot regard that behavior as being an act of mine, unless I further believe that I was the cause of that external or internal event. My pulse, for example, is caused and regulated by certain conditions existing within me, and not by myself. I do not, accordingly, regard this activity of my body as my action, and would be no more tempted to do so if I became suddenly conscious within myself of those conditions or impulses that produce it. This is behavior with which I have nothing to do, behavior that is not within my immediate control, behavior that is not only not free activity, but not even the activity of an agent to begin with; it is nothing but a mechanical reflex. Had I never learned that my very life depends on this pulse beat, I would regard it with complete indifference, as something foreign to me, like the oscillations of a clock pendulum that I idly contemplate.

Now this conception of activity, and of an agent who is the cause of it, involves two rather strange metaphysical notions that are never applied elsewhere in nature. The first is that of a *self* or *person* —for example, a man—who is not merely a collection of things or events, but a substance and a self-moving being. For on this view it is a man himself, and not merely some part of him or something within him, that is the cause of his own activity. Now we certainly do not know that a man is anything more than an assemblage of physical things and processes, which act in accordance with those laws that describe the behavior of all other physical things and processes. Even though a man is a living being, of enormous complexity, there is nothing, apart from the requirements of this theory, to suggest that his behavior is so radically different in its origin from that of other physical objects, or that an understanding of it must be sought in some metaphysical realm wholly different from that appropriate to the understanding of nonliving things.

Second, this conception of activity involves an extraordinary conception of causation, according to which an agent, which is a substance and not an event, can nevertheless be the cause of an event. Indeed, if he is a free agent then he can, on this conception, cause an event to occur —namely, some act of his own—without anything else causing him to do so. This means that an agent is sometimes a cause, without being an antecedent sufficient condition; for if I affirm that I am the cause of some act of mine, then I am plainly not saying that my very existence is sufficient for its occurrence, which would be absurd. If I say that my hand causes my pencil to move, then I am saying that the motion of my hand is, under the other conditions then prevailing, sufficient for the motion of the pencil. But if I then say that I cause my hand to move, I am not saying anything remotely like this, and surely not that the motion of my self is sufficient for the motion of my arm and hand, since these are the only things about me that are moving.

This conception of the causation of events by beings or substances that are not events is, in fact, so different from the usual philosophical conception of a cause that it should not even bear the same name, for "being a cause" ordinarily just means "being an antecedent sufficient condition or set of conditions." Instead, then, of speaking of agents as *causing* their own acts, it would perhaps be better to use another word entirely, and say, for instance, that they *originate* them, *initiate* them, or simply that they *perform* them.

Now this is on the face of it a dubious conception of what a man is. Yet it is consistent with our data, reflecting the presuppositions of deliberation, and appears to be the only conception that is consistent with them, as determinism and simple indeterminism are not. The theory of agency avoids the absurdities of simple indeterminism by conceding that human behavior is caused, while at the same time avoiding the difficulties of determinism by denying that every chain of causes and effects is infinite. Some such causal chains, on this view, have beginnings, and they begin with agents themselves. Moreover, if we are to suppose that it is sometimes up to me what I do, and understand this in a sense which is not consistent with determinism, we must suppose that I am an agent or a being who initiates his own actions, sometimes under conditions which do not determine what action he shall perform. Deliberation becomes, on this view, something that is not only possible but quite rational, for it does make sense to deliberate about activity that is truly my own and that depends in its outcome upon me as its author, and not merely upon something more or less esoteric that is supposed to be intimately associated with me, such as my thoughts, volitions, choices, or whatnot.

One can hardly affirm such a theory of agency with complete comfort, however, and wholly without embarrassment, for the conception of men and their powers which is involved in it is strange indeed, if not positively mysterious. In fact, one can hardly be blamed here for simply denying our data outright, rather than embracing this theory to which they do most certainly point. Our data—to the effect that men do sometimes deliberate before acting, and that when they do, they presuppose among other things that it is up to them what they are going to do—rest upon nothing more than fairly common consent. These data might simply be illusions. It might in fact be that no man ever deliberates, but only imagines that he does, that from pure conceit he supposes himself to be the master of his behavior and the author of his acts. Spinoza has suggested that if a stone, having been thrown into the air, were suddenly to become conscious, it would suppose itself to be the source of its own motion, being then conscious of what it was doing but not aware of the real cause of its behavior. Certainly men are *sometimes* mistaken in believing that they are behaving as a result of choice deliberately arrived at. A man might, for example, easily imagine that his embarking upon matrimony is the result of the most careful and rational deliberation, when in fact the causes, perfectly sufficient for that behavior, might be of an entirely physiological, unconscious origin. If it is sometimes false that we deliberate and then act as the result of a decision deliberately arrived at, even when we suppose it to be true, it might always be false. No one seems able, as we have noted, to describe deliberation without metaphors, and the conception of a thing's being "within one's power" or "up to him" seems to defy analysis or definition altogether, if taken in a sense which the theory of agency appears to require.

These are, then, dubitable conceptions, despite their being so well implanted in the commonsense of mankind. Indeed, when we turn to the theory of fatalism, we shall find formidable metaphysical considerations which appear to rule them out altogether. Perhaps here, as elsewhere in metaphysics, we should be content with discovering difficulties, with seeing what is and what is not consistent with such convictions as we happen to have, and then drawing such satisfaction as we can from the realization that, no matter where we begin, the world is mysterious and the men who try to understand it are even more so. This realization can, with some justification, make one feel wise, even in the full realization of his ignorance.

FATE

5

We all, at certain dramatic moments of pain, threat, or bereavement, entertain the idea of fatalism, the thought that what is then happening just had to be, that we are powerless to prevent it. Sometimes we find ourselves in circumstances not of our own making, circumstances in which our destinies and our very being are thoroughly anchored, and then the thought of fatalism can be quite overwhelming and sometimes consoling. Whatever then happens, one feels, and however good or ill, will be what those circumstances yield, and we are helpless. There is nothing for you or me to do about it, hence nothing for us to think or deliberate about; we can only wait and see. Soldiers, it is said, are sometimes possessed by such thoughts. Perhaps all men would feel more inclined to such thoughts if they paused to think more often of how little they ever had to do with bringing themselves to wherever they have arrived in life, of how much their fortunes and destinies were decided for them by sheer circumstance, and how the entire course of their lives is often set, once for all, by the most trivial incidents, which they did not produce and could not even have foreseen. If we are free to work out our destinies at all, which is doubtful, it is a freedom that is at best exercised within exceedingly narrow paths. The important things—when we are born, of what parents, into what culture, of what sex and temperament, of what intelligence or stupidity, indeed everything that makes for the bulk of our happiness and misery —is decided for us by the most casual and indifferent circumstances, by sheer coincidences, chance encounters, and seemingly insignificant fortuities. One can see this in retrospect if he searches, but few search to find it. The fate that has given us our very being and human natures has thereby made us so that, being human, we congratulate ourselves on our blessings, which we can deem our achievements, blame the world for our deficiencies, which we call our ill luck, and scarcely think of the fate which arbitrarily dispenses both.

Fatalism and determinism   A theory of fatalism is often distinguished academically from the theory of determinism by noting that, whereas determinism is a theory about all things and events, fatalism is a theory about some events only; the theory, namely, that these events could never have been otherwise, regardless of whatever else happened; or that certain events are such that they cannot fail to occur, no matter what else occurs. But this distinction is only academic. A determinist is simply, if he is consistent, a fatalist about everything; or at least, he should be. For the essential idea that a man would be expressing by saying that his attitude was one of fatalism with respect to this or that event—his own death, for instance—is that it is not up to him whether, or when or where, this event will occur, that it is not within his control. But the theory of determinism, as we have seen, once it is clearly spelled out and not hedged about with unresolved "ifs," entails that this is true of everything that ever happens, that it is never really up to any man what he does or what he becomes, and that nothing ever can happen, except what does in fact happen. One can indeed find verbal formulas for distinguishing the two theories, but if we think of a fatalist as one who has a certain attitude toward certain events, we find that it is the attitude that a thoroughgoing believer in determinism should, in consistency, assume toward all events.

Fatalism with respect to the future and the past   A fatalist is best thought of, quite simply, as someone who thinks he cannot do anything about the future. He thinks it is not up to him what will happen next year, tomorrow, or the very next moment. He thinks that even his own behavior is not in the least within his power, any more than the motions of distant heavenly bodies, the events of remote history, or the political developments in faraway countries. He supposes, accordingly, that it is pointless for him to deliberate about anything, for a man deliberates only about those future things he believes to be within his power to do and forego. He does not pretend always to know what will happen. Hence, he might try sometimes to read signs and portents, or contemplate the effects upon him of the various things that might, for all he knows, be fated to occur. But he does not suppose that, whatever will happen, it will ever have been really avoidable.

A fatalist, then, thinks of the future in the manner in which we all think of the past, for all men are fatalists as they look *back* upon things. He thinks of both past and future "under the aspect of eternity," the way God is supposed to view them. We all think of the past in this way, as something once for all settled and fixed, to be taken for just what it is. We are never in the least tempted to modify it, or even to suppose that we ever can. We all believe that it is not in the least now up to us what happened last year, yesterday, or even a moment ago; that these things are no longer within our power, any more than the motions of the heavens or the political developments in China. And of course we are not ever tempted to deliberate about what we have done or left undone. At best we can speculate on these things, try to figure out what they were in case we do not know, or we can rejoice over them or repent. If we are not fatalists about the future, we can extract lessons from the past to apply in the future. But as for what has in fact happened, we do, and feel we certainly must, simply take it as given. The possibilities for action, if there are any at all, do not lie there. We might, indeed, believe that some past things *were* once within our power, to do or avoid, while they were still future—but this expresses our attitude toward the future, not the past.

Such is surely our conception of the whole past, whether near or remote. But the true fatalist thinks of the future in just the same way. We all think things past are no longer within our power; the fatalist thinks they never were. It is a consoling doctrine, as many contemplative minds have discovered; but it somehow seems to violate the common sense of the greater part of mankind.

There are various ways in which one might get thinking fatalistically about the future, but they are most apt to arise from certain theological ideas, or from the metaphysical theory of determinism. Thus, if God is really all-knowing and all-powerful, then it is not hard to suppose that he has already arranged for everything to happen just as it is going to happen, and there is nothing left for you and me to do about it, except to watch things unfold and see what is to become of us, in the here or hereafter. Religious systems have used this thought as a cornerstone, and it is a firm one indeed for those who have this kind of faith. But without bringing God into the picture, it is not hard to suppose, as we have seen, that everything that happens is wholly determined by what went before it, and hence that whatever happens at any future time is the only thing that can then happen, given that certain other things will happen just before then, and that these, in turn, are the only things that can happen then, given the state of the world just before that, and so on, through the infinite past. So again, there is no more left for us to do about what is to be than about what already has been. What we do in the meantime will, to be sure, determine how some things eventually turn out; but these things that we are going to do will, on this conception, be only the causal consequences of what will be happening just before we do them, and so on back to a not distant point at which it seems obvious that we have nothing to do with what happens then.

No man needs convincing that fatalism is the only proper attitude to hold toward things past, but we want to see whether we should think in the same way of the future. The consequences of doing so are obviously momentous. To say nothing of the consolation of fatalism—a consolation which enables one to view all things as they arise, with the same undisturbed mind with which he contemplates even the horrors of remote history—the attitude of fatalism relieves one's mind of all tendency toward both blame and approbation of others and of both guilt and conceit in himself. It promises one that a perfect understanding of everything is at least possible, even if never actually possessed. This thought alone, once firmly grasped, yields a sublime complacency toward everything that life offers, whether to oneself or to his fellows; and while it thereby reduces one's pride, it simultaneously enhances the feelings, opens the heart, and enormously broadens one's understanding.

Presuppositions   Like any metaphysical theory, the theory of fatalism cannot be evaluated apart from one's presuppositions or data. Theological conceptions obviously cannot be invoked here, for they are far more doubtful than any metaphysical theory that one might try to erect on them. At best, they could only serve to convey the theory of fatalism more easily to an unphilosophical imagination. Similarly, the theory of determinism will be of no use to us, for it is not a datum but a theory, and a controversial one too.

For our data we shall use only six claims, each of which recommends itself to the ordinary understanding as soon as it is understood, and hardly any of which have very often been doubted even by the most critical philosophical minds, many of whom, however, have failed to see their implications. These six suppositions, with some explanation of each, are simply these.

First, we suppose that any proposition or statement whatever is either true or, if not true, then false. If anyone affirms anything whatever, as distinguished from merely uttering nonsense, then what he affirms is, if not false, true; and if not true, false. There is no middle ground. This is simply the standard interpretation (*tertium non datur*) of what is called in logic "the law of excluded middle." It has generally been thought to be a necessary truth, and an indisputable law of logical thought. It seems, in any case, quite unexceptionable.

Second, we suppose that if any change or state of affairs is *sufficient* for the occurrence of some other change or state of affairs at the same or any other time, then the former cannot occur without the latter occurring also, even though the two are logically unconnected. This is simply the standard way in which the concept of *sufficiency* is explained in philosophy. A perhaps clearer way of saying the same thing is that if one state of affairs *ensures* another, then the former cannot exist without the other occurring too. The ingestion of cyanide, for instance, ensures death under certain familiar circumstances, which only means that one cannot normally swallow cyanide without dying, even though it is not logically impossible to do so.

Third, we suppose that if any change or state of affairs is *necessary* for some other change or state of affairs at the same or any other time, then the latter cannot occur without the former occurring too, even though they are logically unconnected. This is simply the standard way in which the concept of a *necessary condition* is explained in philosophy. A perhaps clearer way of saying the same thing is that if one state of affairs is *essential* for another, then the latter cannot occur without it. Oxygen, for instance, is essential for life, which means that we cannot normally live without it, even though it is not logically impossible that we should.

Fourth, we suppose that if some change or state of affairs is sufficient for (ensures) another, then that other is necessary (essential) for it; and conversely, if some change or state of affairs is necessary (essential) for another, then that other is sufficient for (ensures) it. This is simply a logical consequence of our second and third data; it follows from the definitions themselves.

Fifth, we suppose that no agent can perform any given action if there is lacking, at the same or any other time, some condition or state of affairs necessary for the occurrence of that act. This follows simply from the idea of anything being necessary or essential for the accomplishment of something else. For example, I cannot live without oxygen, or swim five miles without ever having been in water, or win a certain election without having been nominated, or fly to the moon without some sort of rocket, and so on, for these are all conditions that are necessary, or essential, for doing the things in question. Something is always necessary for the accomplishment of anything at all, and without the thing that is needed, nothing can be done. This is no law of logic, and in fact cannot be expressed even in the contemporary modal logics, but it is nonetheless manifestly true.

And *sixth*, we suppose that time is not "efficacious," that is, that the mere passage of time does not augment or diminish the powers or capacities of anything and, in particular, that it does not enhance or decrease an agent's powers or abilities. This means that if any substance or agent gains or loses powers or abilities over the course of time, then such a gain or loss is always due to something other than the mere passage of time. For instance, if a substance loses or gains in its power to corrode things, or if a man loses or gains the power to do push-ups, or lift weights, or what not, then such gains and losses are always due to certain things that happen over the course of time. They are not due *merely* to the passage of time alone, which has no causal effect upon anything. This cannot be proved, but it is never doubted in physical science, and can hardly be doubted by anyone who thinks on it.

With these data before us, we are now going to compare two simple situations in turn. The relations involved in both situations will be identical except for certain relations of time, and we want to see whether an examination of each situation warrants similar inferences in both cases.

The first   Let us assume that I am going to open my morning newspaper
situation   and glance over the headlines. There have for weeks been rumors of an impending naval battle, and I am intensely interested to learn from the paper whether any such battle has occurred. I have a son who is a sailor, we may suppose, and I am anxious for his safety. Assume further, then, that conditions are such that only if there was such a battle yesterday does my newspaper carry a certain kind of headline—i.e., that such a battle is, in the sense defined, necessary or essential for that kind of headline—whereas if it carries a certain different sort of headline, this will ensure that there was no such battle. Of course newspapers are not always that reliable, but we shall suppose that this one is, at least this time.

Now then, I am about to perform one or the other of two acts; namely, seeing a headline of the first kind or seeing one of the second kind. We shall call these alternative possible acts S and S' respectively. And let us call the two propositions; "A naval battle occurred yesterday" and "No naval battle occurred yesterday," P and P' respectively. We can now assert that if I perform act S, then my doing so will ensure that there was a naval battle yesterday (i.e., that P is true), whereas if I perform S' then my doing that will ensure that no such battle occurred (or, that P' is true). This logically follows from the description of the situation.

With reference to this example, then, let us now ask whether it is up to me which sort of headline I read as I open the newspaper. More precisely, let us consider whether the following statement is true:

(A) It is now within my power to do S, and it is also now within my power to do S'.

It seems quite obvious that this is not true. For if both these acts were equally within my power, that is, if it were up to me which one to do, then it would also be up to me whether or not a naval battle has taken place yesterday, giving me a power over the past which I plainly do not possess. It will be well, however, to express this point in the form of a proof, as follows:

Argument I:
1. If P is true, then it is not within my power to do S' (for in case P is true, then there is, or was, lacking a condition essential for my doing S', the condition, namely, of there being no naval battle yesterday).
2. But if P' is true, then it is not within my power to do S (for a similar reason).
3. But either P is true or P' is true.
∴4. Either it is not within my power to do S, or it is not within my power to do S';

and A is accordingly false. A common-sense way of expressing this is to say that what sort of headline I see depends, among other things, on whether a naval battle took place yesterday, and that in turn is not now up to me.

Now this conclusion is perfectly in accordance with common sense, for we all are, as noted, fatalists with respect to the past. We sometimes try to find out what has happened by reading newspapers and so on, but no one ever supposes that he can determine or in any way influence what has happened, or that the past is in any way within his power to control. We simply have to take past things as they have happened and make the best of them.

It is significant to note incidentally that in the hypothetical sense in which statements of human power or ability are often formulated by philosophers, one *does* have power over the past. For we can surely assert that *if* I do S, this will ensure that a naval battle occurred yesterday; whereas *if*, alternatively, I do S', this will equally ensure the nonoccurrence of such a battle, for these acts are, in the conditions assumed in our example, quite sufficient for the truth of P and P' respectively. Or we can say that I can ensure the occurrence of such a battle yesterday simply by doing S, and that I can ensure its nonoccurrence simply by doing S'. Indeed, if I should ask *how* I can go about ensuring that no naval battle occurred yesterday, perfectly straightforward instructions can be given; namely, the instruction to do S' and by all means to avoid doing S. But of course the hitch is that I cannot do S' *unless* P' is true, the occurrence of the battle in question rendering me quite powerless to do it.

Now let us imagine that I am a naval commander about to issue my order of the day to the fleet. We assume, further, that within the totality of other conditions prevailing, my issuing of a certain kind of order will ensure that a naval battle will occur tomorrow, whereas if I issue another kind of order this will ensure that no such battle occurs.

Now then, I am about to perform one or the other of these two acts; namely, one of issuing an order of the first sort or one of the second sort. We shall call these alternative possible acts O and O′ respectively. And let us call the two propositions "A naval battle will occur tomorrow" and "No naval battle will occur tomorrow," Q and Q′ respectively. We can now assert that if I do act O, then my doing such will ensure that there will be a naval battle (i.e., that Q is true), whereas if I do O′ my doing that will ensure that no naval battle will occur (or, that Q′ is true).

With reference to this example, then, let us now ask whether it is up to me which sort of order I issue. More precisely, let us consider whether the following statement is true:

> (B) It is now within my power to do O, and it is also now within my power to do O′.

Anyone except a fatalist would surely want to say that, in the situation we have envisaged, this statement might well be true; that is, that each of these acts is quite within my power. In the circumstances we assume to prevail, it is, one would think, up to me as the commander whether the naval battle occurs tomorrow or not. It depends only on what kind of order I issue, given all the other conditions as they are; and what kind of order is issued is something for me to decide, something wholly within my power. It is precisely the denial that such statements are ever true that renders one a fatalist.

But we have, alas, exactly the same argument to show that B is false that we had for proving the falsity of A; namely:

Argument II:
1. If Q is true, then it is not within my power to do O′ (for in case Q is true, then there is, or will be, lacking a condition essential for my doing O′, the condition, namely, of there being no naval battle tomorrow).
2. But if Q′ is true, then it is not within my power to do O (for a similar reason).
3. But either Q is true or Q′ is true.
∴ 4. Either it is not within my power to do O, or it is not within my power to do O′;

and *B* is accordingly false. Another way of expressing this is to say that what kind of order I issue depends, among other things, on whether a naval battle takes place tomorrow—for in this situation a naval battle tomorrow is a necessary condition of my doing O, whereas no naval battle tomorrow is equally essential for my doing O'.

In view of the fact that probably everything anyone does, and certainly everything of any significance that anyone ever does, has consequences for the future, so that, his act being sufficient for those consequences, they are in turn necessary conditions of his act, we can generalize upon this conclusion by saying that, for any such act A, either it is not within one's power to do A, or it is not within his power to refrain from doing it, depending of course on which consequences are in fact going to ensue.

At this point most persons are apt to feel most intensely that something has gone wrong, that a piece of sophistry has been concocted merely to puzzle and bewilder; but this is only because most persons are not fatalists about the future. No one feels the slightest suspicion about the first argument. Indeed, the logic of it seems so obvious that one might well wonder what can be the point of spelling it all out so exactly. But that is because everyone is already a fatalist about the past— no one supposes it is up to him what has happened, or that past things are still within his power.

The thing to note, however, is that these two arguments are formally identical, except only for tenses. If the occurrence of a naval battle yesterday is a necessary condition of my reading a certain kind of headline today, then it logically follows that my reading that headline today is a sufficient condition for the prior occurrence of that battle. This is obvious and indisputable. But, similarly, if my issuing a certain kind of order today is a sufficient condition for the occurrence of a naval battle tomorrow, then the occurrence of that naval battle tomorrow is a necessary condition of my issuing that order. This too is indisputable but somehow not so obvious. If, then, either argument is a good one—and surely the first one is—then the other is just as good no matter how anyone might feel about its conclusion.

People do nevertheless seem to have an almost deathless conviction that fatalism about the future has got to be false, though no one, it seems, has ever given a very good reason for thinking so. Men do, as we noted when considering the theory of determinism, have a conviction that future things are within their control, that what is going to happen is somehow up to them, at least sometimes. What they have failed to note, and what it in fact takes considerable sophistication to see, is that the very reasons that can be given for being a fatalist about the past can be given for being a fatalist about the future. Similarly, whatever arguments can be given for rejecting fatalism with respect to the future turn out to be just as conclusive for rejecting it with respect to the past. This is a consequence of the fact that the relations of necessity and sufficiency are perfectly timeless, and hold in exactly the same way, whether from past to future or from future to past, together with the fact that time, by itself, makes no difference to things.

Fatalism is nevertheless an odious philosophy to most persons. It is repellent only to the will, however, and not to the intellect, for men's wills do not normally crave the serenity to which a fatalist is rightly entitled upon his doctrine. Still, the question can only be settled by intelligence, and we shall therefore consider the arguments against this view that some persons are always eager to press.

Considerations of time   It may be tempting, for example, to suggest that perhaps time makes a difference, so that no state of affairs can be necessary for any other *before* that state of affairs exists. But this escape from fatalism is closed by both our fifth and sixth data. Surely if some state of affairs at *any* given time, whether past, present, or future, is necessary for the occurrence of something else, and that state of affairs does not in fact exist *at the time it is needed*, then nothing anyone does can be of the slightest avail in bringing about that occurrence for which it is necessary. To deny this would be equivalent to saying that I can do something now which is sufficient for, or which ensures, the occurrence of something else in the future, *without* getting that future occurrence as a result. This is absurd in itself, and contrary to our second datum. If anyone were to suggest, in spite of this, that a state of affairs that exists *not yet* cannot, just because of that temporal removal, be a necessary condition of anything existing prior to it, this would be logically equivalent to saying that no present state of affairs can ensure another subsequent to it, which is manifestly absurd. We could with equal justice say that a state of affairs, such as yesterday's naval battle, which exists *no longer*, cannot be a necessary condition of anything existing subsequently, there being the same temporal interval here; and that would be arbitrary and false. All that is needed, to restrict the powers that I imagine myself to have to do this thing or that, is that some condition essential to my doing it *does* not, *did* not, or *will* not occur.

Nor can anyone wriggle out of fatalism by representing this sort of situation as one in which there is a simple loss of ability or power resulting from the passage of time. It is one of our data, and a fairly obvious one, that the mere passage of time does not enhance or diminish the powers or abilities of anything. It would be idle to say that I have the power to do O' until, say, tomorrow's naval battle occurs, or the power to do O until tomorrow arrives and we find no naval battle occurring, and so on. What restricts the range of my power to do this thing or that is not the mere *temporal* relations between my acts and certain other states of affairs, but the very existence of those states of affairs themselves. And according to our very first datum, the fact of tomorrow's containing or lacking a naval battle, as the case may be, is already no less a fact than yesterday's containing or lacking one. If at any time I lack the power to perform a certain act, it can only be the result of something, other than the passage of time, that has happened, is happening, or will happen. The fact that there is going to be a naval battle tomorrow, if it is a fact at all, just as surely suffices to render me unable to do O', as the fact that there has been one yesterday, if it is a fact, suffices to render me unable to do S'. The nonoccurrence of those things is, by our very descriptions of the two situations, essential for my doing those things.

Causation   It will not help in the least here to appeal to any particular analysis of causation, or to the fact, if indeed it is one, that causes only "work forward" and not backward. Our problem has been formulated without any reference whatever to causation. It may well be, for all we know, that causal relations have an unalterable direction in time, which is an unclear claim itself; but if so this is perfectly irrelevant, for it is very certain that the relations of necessity and sufficiency between changes and states of affairs do not, and it is in terms of these relations alone that our data and our examples have been described.

Ability   The most philosophically sophisticated criticism of fatalistic arguments of the kind here presented, and one which is centuries old, amounts essentially to denying our fifth datum, to the effect that no agent is able to perform any given act in the absence of some condition necessary for its accomplishment. It is often claimed that all this means, really, is that it is impossible, as a simple matter of logic, *both* that an agent should perform a certain act, *and* that there should be lacking some condition necessary for his doing that act. From this it does not follow, it is claimed, that the agent is *unable* to do that act, but only, that he *does not* do it—and this is perfectly consistent with his still having the ability to do it.

Thus, a gymnast does not lift a weight if he has no weight to lift, but the absence of this necessary condition for lifting a weight does not diminish his strength or his ability to lift weights. Indeed, if the presence of a weight were a necessary condition, not merely of his lifting it, but of his *ability* to lift it, then it would logically follow that his mere ability to lift it would be a sufficient condition for a weight's being present, that his strength would by itself guarantee the perpetual presence of a weight! Gymnasts are sometimes able to lift weights even when none are present, just as musicians are able to make music even when they are not doing so, and horsemen are able to ride horses even when they are walking. The argument for fatalism is, then, it is suggested, a simple *non sequitur*.

Now all this is true in the usual sense of ability, which consists in having the skill, strength, equipment, or knowing how. But to make that point is really to miss the point. If there is lacking some condition C, necessary for my doing a certain act A, or which is such that A cannot occur without it, then not only do I not do A, I *cannot* do it, no matter what my natural or acquired abilities might be. This is perfectly obvious when one considers necessary conditions which are lacking in the past. It should be no less obvious when one considers necessary conditions which are lacking in the future.

For example, we noted that if conditions are such that a naval battle yesterday is a necessary condition for there being a certain kind of headline today, then, given that no such battle occurred, we can conclude not only that I *do not* read such a headline, but that I *cannot*, that it is not within my power, for there is just no such headline for me to read. This is perfectly consistent with my *knowing how* to read it, having the requisite skill and vision, and so on, and thus being able in *that* sense. But if it were within my power to read such a headline, then it logically follows that it would be within my power to make a naval battle occur yesterday which, we are supposing, did not occur; and this is manifestly absurd.

If, accordingly, we were to take the present criticism as a good refutation of fatalism with respect to the future, then it would be just as good a refutation of fatalism about the past, which would be a most extraordinary outcome. For in the sense of ability that this criticism rests upon—namely, the sense of having a certain skill, strength, equipment, or knowing how—we *do* have the ability to change the past. I have the *ability* to read a certain kind of headline—my vision is all right, I know how to read, and so on—and hence am able to do something sufficient for the occurrence of a naval battle yesterday, even though there was no such battle, and therefore some condition is lacking, necessary for there being any such headline for me to read.

Now this observation plainly does not refute fatalism with respect to the past. Sometimes one is prevented from doing what he has the ability to do. Similarly, one cannot, by exploiting this sense of ability, refute fatalism with respect to the future. Just as my knowing how to read does not give me the power to make a battle occur yesterday which did not then occur, so also a man's knowing how to issue an order does not give him the power to make a battle occur tomorrow which will not then occur. The argument for fatalism about the future is just as good as the argument for fatalism about the past; and the argument against either is no better than the argument against the other, the arguments being, in fact, in both cases the same.

**The law of
excluded middle**

There is, of course, one other way one might try to avoid fatalism, and that would be simply to deny one of the premises in Argument II. It is not easy to see how one could do this without embarrassment so long as he accepted the premises of Argument I, for the premises of both arguments are formally identical except for time; but let us not press that.

The first two hypothetical premises can in any case not be rejected without at the same time rejecting every one but the first, and perhaps the last, of our six original data; that would surely be too great a price. Not one of those four data seems the least doubtful. And the third premise of Argument II—that either Q is true, or Q' is true—could be denied only by rejecting the first of our data; that is, by rejecting the very law of excluded middle itself, according to its usual interpretation.

This last escape has, however, been sometimes attempted, particularly by theologians who have been anxious to preserve the omniscience of God even in the face of its plainly fatalistic implications. Let us see whether it promises any real hope of escape.

According to this view, the third premise of Argument II, "either Q is true or Q' is true," or equivalently, "either Q is true or not-Q is true" or, also equivalently, "either Q is true or Q is false," is an instance of the law of excluded middle, and is a necessary truth. Neither of its parts, however—that is, neither Q, nor Q'—is a necessary truth, nor, indeed, even a truth, but is instead a mere "possibility" or "contingency." And, it is sometimes claimed, there is no real absurdity in supposing that two statements, neither of them true and neither of them false, but each of them "possible," might combine into a disjunctive statement which is a necessary truth—for that statement, if it is a disjunction, as this one is, might exhaust the "possibilities."

Now as a matter of fact, if we provisionally assume the *truth* of B, as the nonfatalist is most anxious to do, and substitute this as our third premise in Argument II, we can render a formally valid argument to prove that a true disjunction of contradictories—that is, an instance of the law of excluded middle—might disjoin statements which are neither true nor false by themselves. Thus:

Argument III:

1. If Q is true, then it is not within my power to do O'.
2. But if Q' is true, then it is not within my power to do O.
3. But it *is* within my power to do O, and it is also within my power to do O'.
4. Q' is not true, and Q is not true.

And to this we can add that, since Q and Q' are logical contradictories, such that if either is false then the other must be true, then Q is not false, and Q' is not false—i.e., that neither of them is true and neither of them false.

This line of thought would, to be sure, enable one to avoid being a fatalist, and it is probably the only way one can avoid it. That it involves rejecting the conventional interpretation of the law of excluded middle that has prevailed for over two thousand years might seem to some persons not too great a price to pay for the avoidance of fatalism. One need not, in any case, reject also the law of contradiction by seeking this means of escape, for the law of contradiction asserts only that, concerning any statement, not both it and its contradictory can be true. And that, of course, is perfectly consistent with the line of thought here suggested.

It does seem odd, however, that the law of excluded middle should be deemed inapplicable to the *future*, according to its traditional interpretation, and nonetheless applicable to the *past*. Indeed, it must be obvious that, as Argument II has been modified to get the more agreeable conclusion of Argument III, so also Argument I could be modified in exactly the same way in order to show us that we should not be such fatalists about the past! No one, of course, would ever find this the least plausible. Indeed, if any philosopher wanted to be a fatalist about the future but a nonfatalist about the past—if, that is, he wanted to maintain that we never have any control at all over what is going to happen, and must simply accept the future for whatever it is, but that we can adjust the past more or less as we please—his argument would be just exactly as good as the one we are here considering. It would, in fact, be the *same* argument, allowing only for a few adjustments of tense.

Temporal efficacy

Worse than this, however, we shall now find that if anyone seeks to avoid fatalism by the device just sketched, he will have to surrender not only the first of our data but also the last, to the effect that time by itself is not efficacious; and this, perhaps, *is* too high a price to pay for a belief that has little to be said in its favor in the first place, beyond the fact that we cherish it.

If some statements about the future are neither true nor false, but all statements about the past are the one or the other, then it follows that time by itself has the power to render true or false certain statements which were hitherto neither. In fact, it is doubtful whether one can in any way avoid fatalism with respect to the future, while conceding that things past are, by virtue of their pastness alone, no longer within our power, without thereby conceding an efficacy to time. *Any* such view must entail that future possibilities, at one time within our power to realize or not, cease to be so *merely* as a result of the passage to time—which is precisely what our sixth datum denies. Indeed, this is probably the whole point in casting doubt upon the law of excluded middle in the first place; namely, to call attention to the status of some future but no past things as mere possibilities, thus denying both their complete factuality and their complete lack of it. If so, then the first and sixth of our data are inseparably linked, and the latter must fall with the former.

The affirmation of fatalism   The remaining alternative is to assert, out of a respect for the law of excluded middle and our other data, together with a willingness to view things under the aspect of eternity, that fatalism is a true doctrine, that statements like *B* are, like *A*, never true in such situations as we have described. Of course it is difficult for men to adjust their attitudes to such a philosophy, but it should not be forgotten that all men do, without even thinking about it, have an utterly fatalistic attitude toward the past, as something they can do nothing about, but must simply accept as it is. The philosophy of fatalism requires only that we extend the same attitude toward things future.

It is, moreover, not at all difficult to explain the difference in men's attitudes toward things future and past, which leads them to call some of the former but never any of the latter "possibilities," and to suppose that it is somehow "up to them" what the future contains. This difference in attitude might result entirely from psychological and epistemological considerations. For example, we happen to *know* more about what the past contains than about what is contained in the future, though there is nothing the least bit necessary in this fact. We are like men placed before a large box, the contents of which are entirely unknown to us. So long as we are left only to speculate and guess on what is in the box, we consider all sorts of things "possible," and those contents assume in our minds an aspect of mystery. But as soon as the box is opened and we see what it contained all along, the alternative things that were thought of as possible are seen to be nothing at all, and never to have been even real possibilities.

We can easily imagine a race of men whose knowledge of the future is comparable to our knowledge of the past, but for whom the past is shrouded in darkness and mystery. Such men would find it perfectly natural to be fatalists about the future, but to think of the past as somewhat mysterious and filled with alternative "possibilities." They would view with the profoundest skepticism any philosophical argument purporting to show them that they cannot do anything about the past, though it would seem entirely natural for them to think of the future this way.

Moreover, our memories happen to extend only to things past, which we have experienced. We have no comparable awareness of things future, which we are going to experience. But this, too, seems not the least bit necessary. It is difficult to see how we could have any awareness ahead of time of things we are not yet experiencing, but it is really no more difficult or mysterious than supposing that we should have an awareness afterward of things we are no longer experiencing— and this sort of awareness we do in fact have, in memories. We *feel* that we have a power to control things future, but this feeling of power over future things can easily be the result of just such psychological and epistemological considerations as we have noted. If there were any men whose knowledge of the past were as fragmentary as our knowledge of the future, and who had highly developed precognition but no memory, they might easily imagine themselves to have the same power to control things, but they would imagine that it extended only to things past, which would, for them, be the only realm of real possibilities. These men would regard statements like A as quite evidently true, and statements like B as so plainly doubtful that, for the majority of them, no metaphysics would ever be permitted which tended to render it plausible; for though we have supposed such men to view time differently from ourselves, we have not supposed them to be better philosophers.

TIME AND BECOMING

6

Few things have seemed more metaphysically puzzling to men than time. Unlike space, and the spatial relations between objects, which have usually seemed simple and easy to understand, time has always been regarded by many philosophers as a dark subject of speculation, fundamentally enigmatic and even incomprehensible. Part of this mystery of time has no doubt resulted from thinking of it as something that *moves*. This has led men, quite naturally, to conceive of time as a great vehicle that carries men and all other things inexorably along to their destinies, and that cannot be stayed or impeded. It is partly out of rebellion against this conception, no doubt, that many metaphysicians have declared time to be unreal, to be some sort of illusion. Indeed, it is almost characteristic of metaphysicians to make this claim. Against the idea of a moving and paradoxical time, they have set the idea of *eternity*, as being that realm wherein things are not carried along to their destinies, wherein there is no changing, decaying, or dying, and wherein what is real is immutably so, with no threat of corruption.

Some similarities between spatial and temporal concepts and relations

Except for the fact that time seems to be something that moves—a characteristic that is often referred to as *temporal passage* and described with such words as "becoming"—space and time are very similar in many ways. This can be seen, first of all, from the fact that many of the same terms can be used and readily understood to express either spatial or temporal relations.

The idea of being at a *place*, for example, can express either a spatial or a temporal idea, or both. If someone speaks of something as existing at Ivy, Virginia, for instance, he names its spatial place, and if he speaks of it as existing on June 12, 1962, he names its place in time. By combining these he gives, quite simply, its location in space and time. A corollary to this is the notion of a *distance* or an *interval*, which is easily used in either a spatial or a temporal sense. New York and Boston are spatially distant from each other, while Plato and Kant are temporally so, since one can speak intelligibly of a long interval of time between these two. An allied notion is that of *being present*, which is, significantly, often used to express either the spatial concept of being *here* or the temporal concept of being *now*, or both. Again, the concept of *length* or *being extended* has a use in both contexts, though this is often overlooked. The expression "a length of time" has, in fact, a common use, and there is no more difficulty in understanding the idea of something's lasting through a certain length of time than the idea of its extending through a certain length of space. The notion of length, in turn, leads to that of *parts*, which can be either spatial or temporal. Distinctions between the spatial parts of things are commonplace, but we sometimes also speak of the parts of a melody, or of a man's life. In fact, anything having temporal length, or duration in time, can be divided into temporal parts. The spatial parts of a thing are sometimes very similar to each other, as in the case of a stone, but so also are the temporal parts of something often quite similar to each other—for instance, those of a gravestone, which is much the same at one time as at another. Finally, it should be noted that the concept of a *physical object* involves both space and time, since any such object has, for instance, both kinds of length or extension and both kinds of parts. Some objects are spatially very small, like dust motes, while others are temporally so, like a flash of lightning, while others are both, and some are neither.

Some comparisons of spatial and temporal properties

If one describes things in terms of such concepts as we have just illustrated he finds, often to his surprise, that the differences between their spatial and temporal relations are not so great as he might have supposed. It is intellectually stimulating and edifying to the understanding to see just how far such comparisons can sometimes be carried. We shall not attempt to render here all the comparisons that can be brought to mind, or to enter into the more difficult ones, but one or two examples will illustrate the point.

It is, for example, sometimes said that no object can be in two places at once, though it can occupy two or more times at one place, and some persons imagine that this expresses a very great and basic difference between the spatial and temporal properties of objects.

There are, however, various ways in which an object can occupy two different times at only one place. It might, for example, simply remain where it is through an interval of time. Again, it might be removed from its place and later returned. Or finally, it might be annihilated and subsequently re-created at the same spot. This latter is quite conceivable, though it doubtless never happens. Now it does at first seem as though nothing corresponding to these situations ever can happen the other way around; that is, that no object can be in two places at one time, and in particular that it cannot be *returned* to a time, or annihilated and re-created at two places and one time. When one tries to imagine situations that might be so described, he almost unavoidably finds himself thinking of two objects instead of one.

What must first be noted, however, is that an object is ordinarily said to be in one place at two times only if it also occupies all the time in between, whether at that same place or another, and it must accordingly have some temporal length. Otherwise, we find that we are talking about two objects and not one. But with a similar proviso, an object surely can be in two places at one time; namely, by occupying the space between them as well. A house, for instance, occupies two places at once, if the places referred to are those of its opposite ends. This is quite obvious in the case of a house that straddles a boundary. It might be tempting to interject here that only *part* of the house is in either place—but then, it must be remembered, it is a different *temporal* part of an object which, at the same place, occupies each of two times.

Now the situation analogous to that of an object which is removed from its place and later returned is more complicated and harder to get clear, but it is perfectly possible. To see this, we need only to give an exact description of an object that is removed from its location in space and later returned to it, rewrite the description substituting spatial terms for temporal ones and vice versa, and then see whether what we have written is the description of anything that can ever happen.

Thus, an exact description of any object, O, which is removed from its place and later returned to it, would be as follows: The object O is at place $_1$ at time $_1$ and also at time $_2$; it endures from time $_1$ through time $_2$, but is *then* (i.e., sometime in that temporal interval) at places other than place $_1$.

Now that is a sufficient description of an object that is returned to its place; that is, any object fulfilling that description is, necessarily, so returned.

Let us now rewrite the description, exchanging all spatial and temporal terms for each other, as follows: The object O is at time $_1$ at place $_1$ and also at place $_2$; it extends from place $_1$ through place $_2$, but is *there* (i.e., somewhere in that spatial interval) at times other than time ₁.

Now this is likewise a sufficient description of an object that is returned to its time; that is, any object fulfilling that description is, necessarily, so returned, for the two descriptions are exactly parallel. But does it describe anything that can happen? It does, for we can think of some widespread physical disturbance, such as an earthquake, which exists simultaneously in two nearby towns and at a different time, earlier or later, somewhere between them. The earthquake, we should accordingly say, is temporally removed from its time and, over a lapse of space, returned to it, since it fits that description.

Now some would want to insist here that more than one object is involved in this example, or even that an earthquake is no proper object at all. But it is an object in every significant way—it has a location in space and time, has interesting properties, such as the property of being destructive, and so on. Nor is it to the point to suggest that, in the example given, more than one such object is involved. The people in the different towns could say, rightly, that they suffered from the same earthquake. Moreover, we can and ordinarily do say that moving about in space does not destroy the identity of a thing; no one would say, for instance, that if a chair is moved from one side of the room to the other and then back again, it thereby becomes a different chair. And so likewise, there is no reason for saying that moving about in time, in the manner suggested, destroys the identity of a thing. In the case of the chair, a temporal continuity is retained between its different temporal parts; it at no time, in the temporal interval in which it is moved, ceases to exist altogether. Similarly, the earthquake retains a spatial continuity between its different spatial parts; it at no place, in the spatial interval in which it moves, ceases to exist altogether. The analogies, then, seem quite complete.

There was, we noted, one other way that an object might conceivably be in the same place at two times, and that would be for it to be annihilated and then re-created at the same place. Some persons might want to regard this as the same object at both times, rather than two very similar objects, despite the lack of temporal continuity in it. But here the analogy is exceedingly simple. We need only to describe an object that exists simultaneously at two places and nowhere between, such as a billiard ball which is at once identically at both sides of the table.

Now what has happened here? Surely, we must say that these are two different billiard balls, however similar to each other they might be, simply on the ground that there is no spatial continuity between them.

If they were spatially connected—by a rod, for instance—we might be entitled to speak of them as parts of one object, but not if such continuity is wholly lacking. But in the former case, too, in which an object is supposedly annihilated and then re-created, there is no temporal continuity; the thing simply ceases to exist altogether, and then begins to exist again. If, accordingly, we are dealing with two similar things in either case, rather than with one thing, then we have as good reason for saying we are dealing with two similar things in the other case as well. One may suit himself whether there is an identity or a diversity of things in either case, but it would be arbitrary indeed to insist that there is an identity in the one case but a diversity in the other, the two situations being exactly analogous.

Such comparisons as these can sometimes be worked out with astonishing results. If, for example, one renders an exact description of an object that *changes places* with another in space, or of one that *approaches* another and then *recedes* from it, he will find that he can also render an exact description of an object that changes places with another in time, or of one that approaches another in time and then recedes from it. One needs only to make the descriptions the same in both cases, except that all spatial concepts are replaced by temporal ones and vice versa. The one thing that needs to be remembered, however, is that whenever one allows for a lapse of time in one description, he must also allow for a lapse of space in the other. If, for instance, a lapse of time is needed for two objects to change places in space, as of course it is, then a lapse of space will be needed for two objects to change places in time.

Temporal passage and becoming
The one thing about time that has always been the greatest stumbling block to comparing it with space, however, is its *passage* or *flow* or, what amounts to the same thing, the characteristic all things seem to have of continuously moving through time. Thus, we speak of future things as *drawing nearer*, of then *becoming* present and, having passed into the present, of *receding* endlessly into an ever growing past. Such expressions as these clearly imply that something is moving, though they do not imply that anything is moving in space, in the usual way things move. In fact, a thing needs only to have a place in time in order to be moving in the manner suggested; for concerning any object that ever exists in time we can say that, until it exists, it draws closer and closer to existing; that while it exists it becomes older; and after it ceases to exist it recedes ever farther into the past.

Now this kind of motion or passage through time, which seems to be such a basic and even necessary characteristic of reality, has always profoundly bewildered philosophers, because it seems to be loaded with absurdities as soon as one begins thinking about it. It has seemed so strange to some thinkers that they have simply declared it to be unreal. Since, moreover, it seems impossible even to think of time apart from the idea of its passage, many metaphysicians have drawn the conclusion that time itself is unreal, and that the passage of things through time is an illusion. This idea is found in some of the earliest metaphysical speculations of the Greeks, and has been almost characteristic of metaphysics ever since.

Let us, however, take it as our datum or starting point that, in some sense, things in time pass into, through, and out of existence. This means that, concerning anything whatever that ever exists, we can say that, until it exists, it draws ever closer to existing; that while it exists it grows older; and that after it ceases to exist it recedes ever farther into the past. This seems to be a logical consequence of saying of anything whatever that it exists in time, or that it exists at some time or other.

No metaphysical theories about time make such passage seem the least less real to those who dwell in it and, as men do, look forward and back in it. Men have both the inherent determination to exist and the intelligence or understanding to realize that their tenure of existence is limited. A man's passage through time is for him, then, an appalling fact. That lifeless things should deteriorate and perish makes no difference anywhere. These things have no will to life and no dread of its passage and cessation. The fact that their duration is finite has no more significance than that their bulk is such. If the world turned lifelessly around, carrying only its atmosphere and lifeless things upon it, its passage through time would be quite without significance, and it would not matter whether it was now turning for the millionth or the thousand millionth time. But a man is aware that his life is something that he *passes through*, and that its end is something that, whether near or remote, is nonetheless surely *approaching*. Whether it is his thousandth or twenty thousandth sunrise that he is seeing makes an overwhelming difference, for it marks the extent of his pilgrimage along a path upon which he can neither pause nor turn back, and which has only one possible destination, which is the cessation of his own being. It marks, in fact, how much is gone, and how much is still left, of his own ebbing existence. Nor is it here the mere prospect of his debility that appalls, for a man would be only partially comforted by the realization that the vigor of his youth could be held a bit longer. It is the fact of *passage* itself, with or without the vigor of youth, that concerns one. A man awaiting certain execution draws no comfort from the fact that he need suffer no decay before death. It is the approach of the latter by itself, and the total calamity of it, that emasculates his hope. It is perhaps worth noting, however, that everyone of us is approaching his end, no less certainly and inevitably than one who has had its date fixed for him.

Pure becoming   Let us use the expression "pure becoming" to designate the passage through time to which all things seem to be subjected, merely by virtue of their being in time. It is aptly callad *pure* becoming because any other kind of change or becoming that anything might undergo *presupposes* this kind of change, whereas this pure becoming presupposes no other change at all. Thus, in order for anything to become red, or square, or larger, or weaker, or whatnot, it must pass through a certain amount of time, which is equivalent to saying that it must *become older*. The fact that something becomes older, however, or that it acquires a greater age than it had, does not entail that it undergoes any other change whatever.

The idea of a thing's becoming older is not always, to be sure, thought of in this metaphysical sense. When we describe something as becoming older we often have in mind certain definite and observable changes. For instance, if we say of a man that he is becoming older, we are apt to be referring to the diminution of his strength or vigor, and so on. Aging is, in this sense, simply a physiological concept, and as used in this way we can speak without absurdity of someone's aging more or less rapidly, or even of his becoming younger.

By *pure becoming*, however, we have in mind becoming older simply in the sense of acquiring a greater age, whether that increase of age is attended by any other changes or not. In this sense a thing can become older without undergoing any other change whatever, for it can simply increase in age from one day to the next. This, then, seems to be a kind of becoming or passing through time that can be asserted of anything whatever that exists in time, for it is a consequence simply of its being in time. A thing can be as stable and unchanging as we care to suppose, and yet this appears to be one change that nothing can elude. Even if something should acquire the attributes of newness, and thus elude the process of aging in that sense, it would still have to become older to do so. If a decaying flower, for instance, resumed the fresh form of a bud, it would in one sense appear to become younger but it would nonetheless become older, for otherwise no meaning could be given to the idea of its *resuming* that form. We could say of such a flower on any given day, whatever might be its form and properties, that it is a day older than it was yesterday, that in the meantime it has *become* older, however new and young it may seem. And this, of course, would mark a change—namely, a change in its age, which it had in time undergone.

Now for anything to be passing through time or becoming older it must, of course, exist. Nonentities do not become older or pass through time, for they are not even in time; nor do real things which once existed but have since ceased, or other real things which will sometime exist but which do not exist yet. Diogenes' cup, for instance, became both old and rusty, but both changes ceased with the cessation of that cup's existence. Yet even things which have ceased to exist, and others which will exist in the future but do not exist yet, undergo a *relational* kind of change which is simply a corollary of pure becoming or passage through time. That is, we can speak of Diogenes' cup as *receding* ever farther into the past. It is more remote from us in time today than it was yesterday, and this is a relational change which it is undergoing. Similarly, the birth of my first grandchild, assuming there will be one, is something that is *drawing closer*, and this is a relational change that something which will, but does not yet exist, is already undergoing. I can look forward to it now, but some day I shall only be able to look back upon it; and this is a change that it will meanwhile have undergone and is even now undergoing, in relation to me. Nor is this merely a change in the manner in which I choose to view it, for it is no matter of my choice at all. Just as I cannot now look forward in anticipation to using Diogenes' cup, since this has forever after—for all future time—ceased to be, so also I cannot now look back in memory to the birth of my first grandchild, since this has forever before—for all past time—not yet come to be.

It seems, moreover, that *times* themselves undergo both kinds of change just described. Any actual time, like any actual being, undergoes the same pure becoming or passage as the latter, and any nonactual past or future time undergoes the same relational change characteristic of nonactual past or future beings. Thus, I can say of *today*, which is an actual time, that it is passing, elapsing, its end drawing closer, that it is becoming older. What was true of it this morning is no longer true of it this evening; and this is no less a change of that day itself, a change of its age, than of any being that exists in that day. Nor does this kind of assertion merely express the trivial truth that at, say, nine o'clock, today is nine hours old, and at ten o'clock an hour older—for that statement is true of days that are *not* becoming older—of yesterday and tomorrow, for example, or any day whatever.

Similarly, just as Diogenes' cup is receding into the past, and the birth of my first grandchild drawing ever closer, so also are the *times* of these doing the same. The time that Diogenes took his last sip from his cup is, like that last sip itself, more remote from us today than it was yesterday, and less so than it will become tomorrow. And this is a relational change, with respect to us and the present time, of that time itself.

The strangeness
of this idea This kind of passage or change is surely very odd, so odd that anyone who thinks about it is apt to feel impelled either to deny outright that it even exists, which amounts to denying the datum with which we began, or else to find alternative ways of expressing it. The idea of pure becoming or temporal passage will seem even more strange, however, in the light of the following considerations.

In the first place, we must note that pure becoming is not only an unobservable change but is compatible with, and in fact entailed by, any change whatever that is observed. If, for instance, we see that something, such as a leaf, is green and then becomes red, or red and then becomes green, we must conclude that it also becomes older, for nothing can become anything at all without becoming older in the process. The conception of something's becoming older, then, is a purely a priori notion, a consequence of its simply being in time. Second, any event is a change, and it is therefore quite odd to think of events as themselves changing. Yet events are in time and have duration; hence, while they last, they become older, and when they have ceased they begin an endless recession into the past, like anything else. Third, all ordinary changes, or instances of things gaining or losing properties, presuppose time. It is exceedingly odd, then, to suppose that times themselves should ever be thought of as changing, unless one is willing to assume a mysterious kind of metaphysical "time" against whose background the ordinary time intervals into which we are born and grow older can themselves come into being and age. Yet we have noted that times do seem to change in the sense of undergoing pure becoming—we can say of today, for instance, which is a time, that it is drawing to a close, and will soon begin receding into the past. And finally, the continual recession of things past, and the advance upon us of things future, is a strange kind of passage for the reason that no *rate* of passage can possibly be assigned to it without making nonsense. We cannot, for instance, sensibly say that Diogenes' cup is receding into the past at the rate of one day every twenty-four hours, or even at the rate of one day for every complete rotation of the earth; but what else can one say?

Confronted with such considerations as these, it is tempting to dismiss the pure becoming or temporal passage of things as an illusion, to say that nothing ever really does change in this sense. If a metaphysician wants to make a case for this, he has abundant materials with which to construct his arguments. This amounts, however, to denying the datum with which we began. Moreover, in case the idea of the passage or flow of time is essential to the very conception of time itself, as it may well be, then to deny that there is any such passage would amount to denying that time is real, or that anything is even in time at all. Ever so many metaphysicians have found this conclusion an agreeable one, but it is hardly in accordance with one of the most basic convictions of mankind. However puzzling it may be to metaphysics, it is very difficult for anyone really to convince himself of the falsity of the idea that the end of his life, for example, whether it be near or remote, is something that is approaching, that it will, alas, become present, and that it will then begin receding into the past. Such a statement is readily understood by everyone, and seems quite certainly to express a fact of some sort. If a prisoner who is awaiting execution is told that the hour of his death is approaching and already near, he realizes that he has learned something of great importance to himself. He knows that there is little left of his life, and that what little is left is becoming increasingly less with every passing moment. His terror at this thought would hardly be relieved by his having it pointed out to him by a metaphysician that this kind of change is very strange and even absurd. However strange and mysterious the passage of time might be, it is sometimes nonetheless appalling.

What is needed, then, is some other way of expressing statements embodying the idea of pure becoming, in such a way as to get rid of this idea altogether without thereby destroying the idea of time as well. This is usually attempted by substituting changeless dates for changing nows and thens, or substituting changeless temporal relations, such as earlier and later, for changing ones, such as past and future. The date of anything, such as one's birth, for instance, never changes, nor do the relations of earlier and later, which anything has to other things, ever change—the changeless date of one's birth is eternally earlier than some things, and later than others.

Now there are, as we shall now see, alternative ways of expressing any statement whatever that embodies the idea of temporal passage or pure becoming. But we shall also find, alas, that whenever we reformulate any statement so as to expurgate from it the idea of pure becoming, we are able to understand it only in the light of some *other* proposition that embodies that very idea. When we then try to expurgate pure becoming from that proposition, we shall find that we are able to do so only by putting it back into the first! Our position is thus comparable to that of a man who can easily get rid of mice in his house if he is willing to put up with cats, and who can also get rid of the cats provided he is willing to tolerate mice, but who cannot be rid of both the cats and the mice at once.

The following four statements, wherein X is used to designate some object or event, and Y designates a particular time or interval of time, all embody the idea of pure becoming.

1. X is growing older.
2. X is receding ever farther into the past.
3. Y is growing older.
4. Y is receding ever farther into the past.

Statements of this form, wherein X and Y are replaced with references to particular things or times, respectively, are typical of all statements of pure becoming. If, accordingly, just these four could be reformulated, so as to express such facts as statements of this form are sometimes made to express, but without the idea of pure becoming in them, then there would probably not be any statement expressing pure becoming which could not be similarly reformulated. We could then claim to have gotten rid of the idea of pure becoming altogether, regarding it as an illusory thing having no reality at all.

Consider, then, our first statement, "X is growing older," said of anything whatever, such as a man or a house. One might suppose this to be equivalent to "X occupies an interval of time," or "X exists for more than an instant," or "X endures," or, to get rid of the verb, to "X has duration."

These are clearly not equivalent to our original assertion, however, for they might all apply to something that is not becoming older at all—to past things, for example, that lasted more than an instant, such as Diogenes' cup. This cup ceased growing older as soon as it ceased to be, and yet no one could deny that it has existence or duration through an interval of time.

What obviously needs to be done, then, is to construe such words as "occupies," "endures," and "exists" as expressing the present tense. This can of course be made quite explicit, either by qualifying each of these statements with "now"—for instance, "X *now* occupies an interval of time"—or by saying, more elaborately, "X occupies an interval of time, and that interval has not yet reached its termination." But as soon as we have made this necessary qualification, we have obviously reintroduced pure becoming, merely transferring it from X to some presently elapsing time! Or to make the same point, we can say of this time, this "now" that must be brought in, either (1) that *it* is drawing to an end, or growing older, in case "now" is taken to mean an elapsing interval, such as a day, which can more than once be called "now"; or (2) that *it* recedes ever farther into the past, in case "now" is taken to refer to some particular instant of time which ceases to be as soon as it is mentioned; or (3) that all past things are receding in relation to *it*, in case "now" is understood as continuously referring to some *new* instant each time it is used. It matters not which way "now" is understood; in any case it must, to be understood at all, be understood either as something that is changing, or else something in relation to which everything else is changing. It must, in short, be understood as a concept of pure becoming.

Similar difficulties confront us if we try to reformulate our second sentence, "X is receding ever farther into the past." This does not mean simply that X is in time, for future things are in time, too, and they are not receding into the past, at least not yet. Nor does it mean "X is in the past," for many things, such as myself, that exist in the past have continued their existence into the present, and it would not (yet) be true to say that I, for instance, am receding into the past. Nor does it help to say "X has its *whole* existence in the past," or to give some name to that past interval of its duration, such as "from July 1 through July 26, 1962." For, as we have seen, we can say of that interval, no less that of X, that *it* is receding into the past, the gap between the present and that interval growing larger just as certainly as the gap between the present and X, it being indeed the same gap. It would seem, in fact, that the notion of this recession is an ingredient in our very conception of the *past*, in which case there is little hope of getting rid of the one by appealing to the other. We have again, then, not expurgated pure becoming, but simply transferred it from some X to some Y, which is the time of X.

It seems apparent that a similar result will reward *any* attempt to reformulate our first two statements. This need not be discouraging, however, for we can apparently always get rid of the pure becoming of *things* by ascribing it to *times.* If we can now get rid of the pure becoming of times, we shall have found a way to rid ourselves of it altogether.

Consider now, then, our third statement, "Y is becoming older," which ascribes pure becoming to some interval of time—to a day, let us suppose. Now this is plainly not equivalent to saying merely that Y *is* an interval of time, such as a day, for not every such interval is becoming older, or elapsing. The day of Diogenes' birth, for instance, is a day, but not one that is elapsing or drawing to an end. Plainly, if Y is a day, then of all the days one might consider, only one of them can be Y, namely, today. Is our original statement, then, on the assumption that Y designates some day, simply equivalent to "Y is today"? It is, but this does not get us far, because the only thing that distinguishes this day from all others is that it is the only one that is drawing to a close, or growing older. So the identification of Y with today does not rid us of that notion. One might try to identify this day in some other manner, e.g., by saying that Y is the day on which X occurs, but that does not work, because it is not necessarily true, of any X, that it occurs on this particular day. "Y is the day on which X occurs" might easily be true, and "Y is becoming older" might be false—indeed, *must* sometimes be false—so the two statements can hardly be equivalent. Nor will it help to identify Y by its date, for it is again unnecessary that today should fall on any particular date. In being told merely that Y is identical with this or that date, I do not know that *today* is Y. If, further, our original sentence is reformulated as "Y is an interval of which an instantaneous *now* is a part," then we only shift the becoming of this interval to the *now* which is a part of it, there being nothing more manifestly fleeting than this. More precisely, we can say of this *now* either (1) that the beginning of Y is receding in relation to it, if "now" is understood as being capable of referring to more than one time; or (2) that this *now* will become a part of a day which is not Y, namely, a part of tomorrow; or (3) that this *now* is itself receding into the past, if "now" is understood as designating only one time. All these statements clearly embody the notion of pure becoming.

Of course similar difficulties will arise in trying to reformulate our last sentence, "Y is receding ever farther into the past," wherein Y refers to an instant or an interval of past time. We cannot just say that Y is the time at which some past X happened, for we were able to get rid of the recession of this X only by transferring it to a time, and this reformulation would only put us back where we started. We might, then, say that Y is entirely a past time—but this does not help either, for we can immediately add that its pastness is something which it *became*, and that it is now becoming increasingly past, there being no past time which has not also been future. The idea of becoming, in short, is part of the very notion of anything's being past, and there is no hope of being rid of that idea by resorting to the concept of pastness.

No other relation, however, will work at all. We cannot just say that Y is *earlier* or *anterior* to some time, for instance, for this is true of all times whatever, including those which are not receding into the past—namely, of all future times. We must identify the time to which Y is anterior, either as being the present time, or some time itself anterior to the present, and the hopelessness of this is quite obvious. The time one would be thus calling "the present time" either has not always been present, but became such—in which case, though Y has indeed always been anterior to it, it is a time which undergoes the same pure becoming as Y—or that if in some sense "the present" time *has* always been the present time, and hence never became such, then plainly Y has not always been anterior to it, but *became* such.

It looks as though a similar failure will reward any attempt to reformulate our last two statements, and any others significantly like them. We seem justified in concluding, then, that the pure becoming of the world and of time is no myth or illusion, however obscure it may be to our reason, and that this strange notion cannot be purged from our understanding of the temporal aspect of things without destroying our very understanding of those things, as being in time.

GOD

7

An active, living, and religious belief in the gods has probably never arisen and been maintained on purely metaphysical grounds. Such beliefs are found in every civilized land and time, and are often virtually universal in a particular culture, yet relatively few men have much of a conception of metaphysics. There are in fact entire cultures, such as ancient Israel, to whom metaphysics is quite foreign, though these cultures may nevertheless be religious.

Belief in the gods seems to have its roots in human desires and fears, particularly those associated with self-preservation. Like all other creatures, men have a profound will to live, which is what mainly gives one's existence a meaning from one sunrise to the next. Unlike other creatures, however, men are capable of the full and terrible realization of their own inevitable decay. A man can bring before his mind the image of his own grave, and with it the complete certainty of its ultimate reality, and against this his will naturally recoils. It can hardly seem to him less than an absolute catastrophe, the very end, so far as he is concerned, of everything, though he has no difficulty viewing death, as it touches others more or less remote from himself, as a perhaps puzzling, occasionally distressing, but nonetheless necessary aspect of nature. It is probably partly in response to this fear that he turns to the gods, as those beings of such power that they can overturn this verdict of nature.

The sources of religious belief are doubtless much more complex than this, but they seem to lie in man's will rather than in his speculative intelligence, nevertheless. Men who possess such a belief seldom permit any metaphysical considerations to wrest it from them, while those who lack it are seldom turned toward it by other metaphysical considerations. Still, in every land in which philosophy has flourished, there have been profound thinkers who have sought to discover some metaphysical basis for a rational belief in the existence of some supreme being or beings. Even though religion may properly be a matter of faith rather than reason, still, a philosophical person can hardly help wondering whether it might, at least in part, be also a matter of reason, and whether, in particular, the existence of God might be something that can be not merely believed but shown. It is this question that we want now to consider; that is, we want to see whether there are not strong metaphysical considerations from which the existence of some supreme and supranatural being might reasonably be inferred.

The principle of sufficient reason   Suppose you were strolling in the woods and, in addition to the sticks, stones, and other accustomed litter of the forest floor, you one day came upon some quite unaccustomed object, something not quite like what you had ever seen before and would never expect to find in such a place. Suppose, for example, that it is a large ball, about your own height, perfectly smooth and translucent. You would deem this puzzling and mysterious, certainly, but if one considers the matter, it is no more inherently mysterious that such a thing should exist than that anything else should exist. If you were quite accustomed to finding such objects of various sizes around you most of the time, but had never seen an ordinary rock, then upon finding a large rock in the woods one day you would be just as puzzled and mystified. This illustrates the fact that something that is mysterious ceases to seem so simply by its accustomed presence. It is strange indeed, for example, that a world such as ours should exist; yet few men are very often struck by this strangeness, but simply take it for granted.

Suppose, then, that you have found this translucent ball and are mystified by it. Now whatever else you might wonder about it, there is one thing you would hardly question; namely, that it did not appear there all by itself, that it owes its existence to something. You might not have the remotest idea whence and how it came to be there, but you would hardly doubt that there was an explanation. The idea that it might have come from nothing at all, that it might exist without there being any explanation of its existence, is one that few people would consider worthy of entertaining.

This illustrates a metaphysical belief that seems to be almost a part of reason itself, even though few men ever think upon it; the belief, namely, that there is some explanation for the existence of anything whatever, some reason why it should exist rather than not. The sheer nonexistence of anything, which is not to be confused with the passing out of existence of something, never requires a reason; but existence does. That there should never have been any such ball in the forest does not require any explanation or reason, but that there should ever be such a ball does. If one were to look upon a barren plain and ask why there is not and never has been any large translucent ball there, the natural response would be to ask why there should be; but if one finds such a ball, and wonders why it is there, it is not quite so natural to ask why it should *not* be, as though existence should simply be taken for granted. That anything should not exist, then, and that, for instance, no such ball should exist in the forest, or that there should be no forest for it to occupy, or no continent containing a forest, or no earth, nor any world at all, do not seem to be things for which there needs to be any explanation or reason; but that such things should be, does seem to require a reason.

The principle involved here has been called the principle of sufficient reason. Actually, it is a very general principle, and is best expressed by saying that, in the case of any positive truth, there is some sufficient reason for it, something which, in this sense, makes it true—in short, that there is some sort of explanation, known or unknown, for everything.

Now some truths depend on something else, and are accordingly called *contingent*, while others depend only upon themselves, that is, are true by their very natures and are accordingly called *necessary*. There is, for example, a reason why the stone on my window sill is warm; namely, that the sun is shining upon it. This happens to be true, but not by its very nature. Hence, it is contingent, and depends upon something other than itself. It is also true that all the points of a circle are equidistant from the center, but this truth depends upon nothing but itself. No matter what happens, nothing can make it false. Similarly, it is a truth, and a necessary one, that if the stone on my window sill is a body, as it is, then it has a form, since this fact depends upon nothing but itself for its confirmation. Untruths are also, of course, either contingent or necessary, it being contingently false, for example, that the stone on my window sill is cold, and necessarily false that it is both a body and formless, since this is by its very nature impossible.

The principle of sufficient reason can be illustrated in various ways, as we have done, and if one thinks about it, he is apt to find that he presupposes it in his thinking about reality, but it cannot be proved. It does not appear to be itself a necessary truth, and at the same time it would be most odd to say it is contingent. If one were to try proving it, he would sooner or later have to appeal to considerations that are less plausible than the principle itself. Indeed, it is hard to see how one could even make an argument for it, without already assuming it. For this reason it might properly be called a presupposition of reason itself. One can deny that it is true, without embarrassment or fear of refutation, but one is then apt to find that what he is denying is not really what the principle asserts. We shall, then, treat it here as a datum—not something that is provably true, but as something which all men, whether they ever reflect upon it or not, seem more or less to presuppose.

The existence It happens to be true that something exists, that there is, for
of a world example, a world, and while no one ever seriously supposes that
this might not be so, that there might exist nothing at all, there still seems to be nothing the least necessary in this, considering it just by itself. That no world should ever exist at all is perfectly comprehensible and seems to express not the slightest absurdity. Considering any particular item in the world it seems not at all necessary in itself that it should ever have existed, nor does it appear any more necessary that the totality of these things, or any totality of things, should ever exist.

From the principle of sufficient reason it follows, of course, that there must be a reason, not only for the existence of everything in the world but for the world itself, meaning by "the world" simply everything that ever does exist, except God, in case there is a god. This principle does not imply that there must be some purpose or goal for everything, or for the totality of all things; for explanations need not, and in fact seldom are, teleological or purposeful. All the principle requires is that there be some sort of reason for everything. And it would certainly be odd to maintain that everything in the world owes its existence to something, that nothing in the world is either purely accidental, or such that it just bestows its own being upon itself, and then to deny this of the world itself. One can indeed *say* that the world is in some sense a pure accident, that there simply is no reason at all why this or any world should exist, and one can equally say that the world exists by its very nature, or is an inherently necessary being. But it is at least very odd and arbitrary to deny of this existing world the need for any sufficient reason, whether independent of itself or not, while presupposing that there is a reason for every other thing that ever exists.

Consider again the strange ball that we imagine has been found in the forest. Now we can hardly doubt that there must be an explanation for the existence of such a thing, though we may have no notion what that explanation is. It is not, moreover, the fact of its having been found in the forest rather than elsewhere that renders an explanation necessary. It matters not in the least where it happens to be, for our question is not how it happens to be *there* but how it happens to exist at all. If we in our imagination annihilate the forest, leaving only this ball in an open field, our conviction that it is a contingent thing and owes its existence to something other than itself is not reduced in the least. If we now imagine the field to be annihilated, and in fact everything else as well to vanish into nothingness, leaving only this ball to constitute the entire physical universe, then we cannot for a moment suppose that its existence has thereby been explained, or the need of any explanation eliminated, or that its existence is suddenly rendered self-explanatory. If we now carry this thought one step further and suppose that no other reality ever has existed or ever will exist, that this ball forever constitutes the entire physical universe, then we must still insist on there being some reason independent of itself why it should exist rather than not. If there must be a reason for the existence of any particular thing, then the necessity of such a reason is not eliminated by the mere supposition that certain other things do *not* exist. And again, it matters not at all what the thing in question is, whether it be large and complex, such as the world we actually find ourselves in, or whether it be something small, simple and insignificant, such as a ball, a bacterium, or the merest grain of sand. We do not avoid the necessity of a reason for the existence of something merely by describing it in this way or that. And it would, in any event, seem quite plainly absurd to say that if the world were comprised entirely of a single ball about six feet in diameter, or of a single grain of sand, then it would be contingent and there would have to be some explanation other than itself why such a thing exists, but that, since the actual world is vastly more complex than this, there is no need for an explanation of its existence, independent of itself.

Beginningless existence   It should now be noted that it is no answer to the question, why a thing exists, to state *how long* it has existed. A geologist does not suppose that he has explained why there should be rivers and mountains merely by pointing out that they are old. Similarly, if one were to ask, concerning the ball of which we have spoken, for some sufficient reason for its being, he would not receive any answer upon being told that it had been there since yesterday. Nor would it be any better answer to say that it had existed since before anyone could remember, or even that it had always existed; for the question was not one concerning its age but its existence. If, to be sure, one were to ask where a given thing came from, or how it came into being, then upon learning that it had always existed he would learn that it never really *came* into being at all; but he could still reasonably wonder why it should exist at all. If, accordingly, the world—that is, the totality of all things excepting God, in case there is a god—had really no beginning at all, but has always existed in some form or other, then there is clearly no answer to the question, where it came from and when; it did not, on this supposition, *come* from anything at all, at any time. But still, it can be asked why there is a world, why indeed there is a beginning-less world, why there should have perhaps always been something rather than nothing. And, if the principle of sufficient reason is a good principle, there must be an answer to that question, an answer that is by no means supplied by giving the world an age, or even an infinite age.

Creation   This brings out an important point with respect to the concept of creation that is often misunderstood, particularly by those whose thinking has been influenced by Christian ideas. People tend to think that creation—for example, the creation of the world by God—*means* creation *in time*, from which it of course logically follows that if the world had no beginning in time, then it cannot be the creation of God. This, however, is erroneous, for creation means essentially *dependence*, even in Christian theology. If one thing is the creation of another, then it depends for its existence on that other, and this is perfectly consistent with saying that both are eternal, that neither ever came into being, and hence, that neither was ever created at any point of time. Perhaps an analogy will help convey this point. Consider, then, a flame that is casting beams of light. Now there seems to be a clear sense in which the beams of light are dependent for their existence upon the flame, which is their source, while the flame, on the other hand, is not similarly dependent for its existence upon them. The beams of light arise from the flame, but the flame does not arise from them. In this sense, they are the creation of the flame; they derive their existence from it. And none of this has any reference to time; the relationship of dependence in such a case would not be altered in the slightest if we supposed that the flame, and with it the beams of light, had always existed, that neither had ever *come* into being.

Now if the world is the creation of God, its relationship to God should be thought of in this fashion; namely, that the world depends for its existence upon God, and could not exist independently of God. If God is eternal, as those who believe in God generally assume, then the world may (though it need not) be eternal too, without that altering in the least its dependence upon God for its existence, and hence without altering its being the creation of God. The supposition of God's eternality, on the other hand, does not by itself imply that the world is eternal too; for there is not the least reason why something of finite duration might not depend for its existence upon something of infinite duration—though the reverse is, of course, impossible.

God   If we think of God as "the creator of heaven and earth," and if we consider heaven and earth to include everything that exists except God, then we appear to have, in the foregoing considerations, fairly strong reasons for asserting that God, as so conceived, exists. Now of course most people have much more in mind than this when they think of God, for religions have ascribed to God ever so many attributes that are not at all implied by describing him merely as the creator of the world; but that is not relevant here. Most religious persons do, in any case, think of God as being at least the creator, as that being upon which everything ultimately depends, no matter what else they may say about him in addition. It is, in fact, the first item in the creeds of Christianity that God is the "creator of heaven and earth." And, it seems, there are good metaphysical reasons, as distinguished from the persuasions of faith, for thinking that such a creative being exists.

If, as seems clearly implied by the principle of sufficient reason, there must be a reason for the existence of heaven and earth—i.e., for the world—then that reason must be found either in the world itself, or outside it, in something that is literally supranatural, or outside heaven and earth. Now if we suppose that the world—i.e., the totality of all things except God—contains within itself the reason for its existence, we are supposing that it exists by its very nature, that is, that it is a necessary being. In that case there would, of course, be no reason for saying that it must depend upon God or anything else for its existence; for if it exists by its very nature, then it depends upon nothing but itself, much as the sun depends upon nothing but itself for its heat. This, however, is implausible, for we find nothing about the world or anything in it to suggest that it exists by its own nature, and we do find, on the contrary, ever so many things to suggest that it does not. For in the first place, anything which exists by its very nature must necessarily be eternal and indestructible. It would be a self-contradiction to say of anything that it exists by its own nature, or is a necessarily existing thing, and at the same time to say that it comes into being or passes away, or that it ever could come into being or pass away. Nothing about the world seems at all like this, for concerning anything in the world, we can perfectly easily think of it as being annihilated, or as never having existed in the first place, without there being the slightest hint of any absurdity in such a supposition. Some of the things in the universe are, to be sure, very old; the moon, for example, or the stars and the planets. It is even possible to imagine that they have always existed. Yet it seems quite impossible to suppose that they owe their existence to nothing but themselves, that they bestow existence upon themselves by their very natures, or that they are in themselves things of such nature that it would be impossible for them not to exist. Even if we suppose that something, such as the sun, for instance, has existed forever, and will never cease, still we cannot conclude just from this that it exists by its own nature. If, as is of course very doubtful, the sun has existed forever and will never cease, then it is possible that its heat and light have also existed forever and will never cease; but that would not show that the heat and light of the sun exist by their own natures. They are obviously contingent and depend on the sun for their existence, whether they are beginningless and everlasting or not.

There seems to be nothing in the world, then, concerning which it is at all plausible to suppose that it exists by its own nature, or contains within itself the reason for its existence. In fact, everything in the world appears to be quite plainly the opposite, namely, something that not only need not exist, but at some time or other, past or future or both, does not in fact exist. Everything in the world seems to have a finite duration, whether long or short. Most things, such as ourselves, exist only for a short while; they come into being, then soon cease. Other things, like the heavenly bodies, last longer, but they are still corruptible, and from all that we can gather about them, they too seem destined eventually to perish. We arrive at the conclusion, then, that while the world may contain some things which have always existed and are destined never to perish, it is nevertheless doubtful that it contains any such thing and, in any case, everything in the world is capable of perishing, and nothing in it, however long it may already have existed and however long it may yet remain, exists by its own nature, but depends instead upon something else.

While this might be true of everything in the world, is it necessarily true of the world itself? That is, if we grant, as we seem forced to, that nothing in the world exists by its own nature, that everything in the world is contingent and perishable, must we also say that the world itself, or the totality of all these perishable things, is also contingent and perishable? Logically, we are not forced to, for it is logically possible that the totality of all perishable things might itself be imperishable, and hence, that the world might exist by its own nature, even though it is comprised exclusively of things which are contingent. It is not logically necessary that a totality should share the defects of its members. For example, even though every man is mortal, it does not follow from this that the human race, or the totality of all men, is also mortal; for it is possible that there will always be human beings, even though there are no human beings which will always exist. Similarly, it is possible that the world is in itself a necessary thing, even though it is comprised entirely of things that are contingent.

This is logically possible, but it is not plausible. For we find nothing whatever about the world, any more than in its parts, to suggest that it exists by its own nature. Concerning anything in the world, we have not the slightest difficulty in supposing that it should perish, or even, that it should never have existed in the first place. We have almost as little difficulty in supposing this of the world itself. It might be somewhat hard to think of everything as utterly perishing and leaving no trace whatever of its ever having been, but there seems to be not the slightest difficulty in imagining that the world should never have existed in the first place. We can, for instance, perfectly easily suppose that nothing in the world had ever existed except, let us suppose, a single grain of sand, and we can thus suppose that this grain of sand has forever constituted the whole universe. Now if we consider just this grain of sand, it is quite impossible for us to suppose that it exists by its very nature, and could never have failed to exist. It clearly depends for its existence upon something other than itself, if it depends on anything at all. The same will be true if we consider the world to consist, not of one grain of sand, but of two, or of a million, or, as we in fact find, of a vast number of stars and planets and all their minuter parts.

It would seem, then, that the world, in case it happens to exist at all—and this is quite beyond doubt—is contingent and thus dependent upon something other than itself for its existence, if it depends upon anything at all. And it must depend upon something, for otherwise there could be no reason why it exists in the first place. Now that upon which the world depends must be something that either exists by its own nature or does not. If it does not exist by its own nature, then it, in turn, depends for its existence upon something else, and so on. Now then, we can say either of two things; namely, (1) that the world depends for its existence upon something else, which in turn depends on still another thing, this depending upon still another, *ad infinitum*; or (2) that the world derives its existence from something that exists by its own nature and which is accordingly eternal and imperishable, and is the creator of heaven and earth. The first of these alternatives, however, is impossible, for it does not render a sufficient reason why anything should exist in the first place. Instead of supplying a reason why any world should exist, it repeatedly begs off giving a reason. It explains what is dependent and perishable in terms of what is itself dependent and perishable, leaving us still without a reason why perishable things should exist at all, which is what we are seeking. Ultimately, then, it would seem that the world, or the totality of contingent or perishable things, in case it exists at all, must depend upon something that is necessary and imperishable, and which accordingly exists, not in dependence upon something else, but by its own nature.

"Self-caused" What has been said thus far gives some intimation of what meaning should be attached to the concept of a self-caused being, a concept that is quite generally misunderstood, sometimes even by scholars. To say that something—God, for example—is self-caused, or is the cause of its own existence, does not mean that this being brings itself into existence, which is a perfectly absurd idea. Nothing can *bring* itself into existence. To say that something is self-caused (*causa sui*) means only that it exists, not contingently or in dependence upon something else, but by its own nature, which is only to say that it is a being which is such that it can neither come into being nor perish. Now whether such a being in fact exists or not, there is in any case no absurdity in the idea. We have found, in fact, that the principle of sufficient reason seems to point to the existence of such a being, as that upon which the world, with everything in it, must ultimately depend for its existence.

"Necessary being" A being that depends for its existence upon nothing but itself, and is in this sense self-caused, can equally be described as a necessary being; that is to say, a being that is not contingent, and hence not perishable. For in the case of anything which exists by its own nature, and is dependent upon nothing else, it is impossible that it should not exist, which is equivalent to saying that it is necessary. Many persons have professed to find the gravest difficulties in this concept, too, but that is partly because it has been confused with other notions. If it makes sense to speak of anything as an *impossible* being, or something which by its very nature does not exist, then it is hard to see why the idea of a necessary being, or something which in its very nature exists, should not be just as comprehensible. And of course, we have not the slightest difficulty in speaking of something, such as a square circle or a formless body, as an impossible being. And if it makes sense to speak of something as being perishable, contingent, and dependent upon something other than itself for its existence, as it surely does, then there seems to be no difficulty in thinking of something as imperishable and dependent upon nothing other than itself for its existence.

"First cause" From these considerations we can see also what is properly meant by a first cause, an appellative that has often been applied to God by theologians, and which many persons have deemed an absurdity. It is a common criticism of this notion to say that there need not be any first cause, since the series of causes and effects which constitute the history of the universe might be infinite or beginningless and must, in fact, be infinite in case the universe itself had no beginning in time. This criticism, however, reflects a total misconception of what is meant by a first cause. *First* here does not mean first in time, and when God is spoken of as a first cause, he is not being described as a being which, at some time in the remote past, *started* everything. To describe God as a first cause is only to say that he is literally a *primary* rather than a secondary cause, an *ultimate* rather than a derived cause, or a being upon which all other things, heaven and earth, ultimately depend for their existence. It is, in short, only to say that God is the creator, in the sense of creation explained above. Now this, of course, is perfectly consistent with saying that the world is eternal or beginningless. As we have seen, one gives no reason for the existence of a world merely by giving it an age, even if it is supposed to have an infinite age. To use a helpful analogy, we can say that the sun is the first cause of daylight and, for that matter, of the moonlight of the night as well, which means only that daylight and moonlight ultimately depend upon the sun for their existence. The moon, on the other hand, is only a secondary or derivative cause of its light. This light would be no less dependent upon the sun if we affirmed that it had no beginning, for an ageless and beginningless light requires a source no less than an ephemeral one. If we supposed that the sun has always existed, and with it its light, then we would have to say that the sun has always been the first—i.e., the primary or ultimate—cause of its light. Such is precisely the manner in which God should be thought of, and is by theologians often thought of, as the first cause of heaven and earth.

The nature   Thus far we have considered nothing about the world except the
of the world   bare fact of its existence, an existence which, it has seemed, is
contingent rather than necessary. It matters not, so far as concerns anything said so far, whether the world is orderly or chaotic, large or small, simple or complex, for the ideas so far elicited would still have whatever force they do have, if any, even if we supposed the world to consist of nothing more than the merest grain of sand.

Many persons, however, have thought that the nature or character of the world and its parts point most clearly to the existence of some supranatural "guiding hand," that is, to some *purposeful* being who, whether he created the world or not, nevertheless fashioned it. What is significant here is not merely that some world or other exists, but rather, that it is the kind of world we find. What we find is not a mere grain of sand, nor a conglomeration of these or similar things, nor a chaos. We find an order and harmony, to say nothing of the mystery and complexity of things that our profoundest science and learning seem only barely to penetrate. Students are sometimes awed by the beautiful machinery and apparently purposeful design of the universe when they receive their initiation to science, whether this is discovered to them in the smallest parts of nature, particularly living things, or in the vastness of the heavens. Of course this orderliness is before our eyes all the time, but we hardly notice it, simply because we are so accustomed to it that we tend to take it for granted. The homeostasis or self-regulation of our own bodies, for instance, whereby the body manages to maintain the most unbelievable internal harmony and to adapt itself to the most diverse and subtle forces acting upon it, represents a wonder which human art cannot really duplicate and our science only dimly comprehends. Yet most men live out their lives without even noticing this seeming miracle that is perpetually before them. The same type of order and seemingly goal-directed change is apparent in the embryological development of living things.

This suggests another feature of the world which, in case it is real and not merely apparent, tends to cast doubt upon the supposition that the world we find ourselves in is the accidental and unintended result of the interacting forces of physical nature; namely, that some things in the world, particularly living organisms, seem purposeful or goal-directed in their very construction. Much modern biology is predicated on the supposition that such seemingly purposeful construction is only apparent and not real; indeed, the main significance of Darwin's work was that he made a convincing case for this. Yet, apart from the requirements of a more or less unconsciously held scientific orthodoxy, it is by no means obvious that this is so. If one considers any living thing whatever, he finds that its powers and construction are perfectly adapted to its mode of life. A hawk, for example, has sharp talons, rapacious beak, keen eyes, strength, and a digestive system all perfectly suited to a predatory mode of life. A lowly spider has likewise precisely what is needed in order to entrap its prey in artfully contrived snares. So it is with every creature whatever. Its anatomy, powers, and instincts are perfectly suited to its goal or mode of life. One can, of course, insist that it is only *because* such beings are so equipped that they pursue the goals that they do, and deny that they are so equipped *in order* to pursue those goals, just as one can insist that it is only *because* a man is carrying rod and reel that he goes fishing, and deny that he is carrying this equipment *in order* to fish; but this seems artificial, even if one gives the evolutionary theory of the origin of such creatures everything that it claims.

The considerations barely adumbrated here fall into a whole

cluster of arguments which are all called, loosely, the argument from design. The common element in them is that they endeavor to establish the existence of some supranatural and creative being or beings from a consideration of the apparently artful and purposeful design manifested in the world, particularly in living things. We cannot go into a discussion of these arguments, for they are already embodied in an abundant literature, and are for the most part inconclusive anyway. There is, however, one way of expressing the argument from design which has a peculiarly rational twist and which has, moreover, been hardly more than dimly perceived by most of those who have considered this subject. It rests upon the consideration that our own faculties of sense and cognition are not only remarkable in themselves but are in fact relied upon by us for the discovery of truth. It is this, and its implications, that we want now to consider.

Chance and evidence   The idea we want to develop here is not easy to grasp without misunderstanding, so it will be best to approach it stepwise by considering first an example or two that should make it quite obvious.

Suppose, then, that you are riding in a railway coach and glancing from the window at one of the stops, you see numerous white stones scattered about on a small hillside near the train in a pattern resembling these letters: THE BRITISH RAILWAYS WELCOMES YOU TO WALES. Now you could scarcely doubt that these stones do not just accidentally happen to exhibit that pattern. You would, in fact, feel quite certain that they were purposefully *arranged* that way to convey an intelligible message. At the same time, however, you could not prove, just from a consideration of their arrangement alone, that they were arranged by a purposeful being. It is possible—at least logically so—that there was no guiding hand at all in back of this pattern, that it is simply the result of the operations of inanimate nature. It is possible that the stones, one by one, rolled down the hill and, over the course of centuries, finally ended up in that interesting arrangement, or that they came in some other accidental way to be so related to each other. For surely the mere fact that something has an interesting or striking shape or pattern, and thus *seems* purposefully arranged, is no proof that it is. There might always be some other explanation. Snowflakes, viewed under magnification, exhibit symmetrical, interesting and often beautiful shapes, and yet we know that these are not designed but can be explained simply in terms of the physics of crystallization. We find *apparently* purposeful arrangements and contrivances around us all the time, but we cannot always conclude that these are in fact the expressions of any purpose. Our own bodies and their organs seem purposeful not only in their individual structures but in their relationships to each other, and yet there are well known theories, resting on such nonpurposeful concepts as chance variation, natural selection, and so on, which are able, at least in the opinion of many learned men, to explain these structures without introducing any ideas of purpose and design at all.

Here, however, is the important point which it is easy to overlook; namely, that *if*, upon seeing from the train window a group of stones arranged as described, you were to conclude that you were entering Wales, and *if* your sole reason for thinking this, whether it was in fact good evidence or not, was that the stones were so arranged, *then* you could not, consistently with that, suppose that the arrangement of the stones was accidental. You would, in fact, be presupposing that they were arranged that way by an intelligent and purposeful being or beings, for the purpose of conveying a certain message having nothing to do with the stones themselves. Another way of expressing the same point is, that it would be *irrational* for you to regard the arrangement of the stones as evidence that you were entering Wales, and at the same time to suppose that they might have come to have that arrangement accidentally, that is, as the result of the ordinary interactions of natural or physical forces. If, for instance, they came to be so arranged over the course of time, simply by rolling down the hill, one by one, and finally just happening to end up that way, or if they were strewn upon the ground that way by the forces of an earthquake or storm or whatnot, then their arrangement would in no sense constitute evidence that you were entering Wales, or for anything whatever unconnected with themselves.

Consider another example. Suppose a stone were dug up and found to be covered with interesting marks, all more or less the same size and more or less in rows. Now there is nothing very remarkable about that. Glaciers and volcanoes have produced stones no less interesting, in abundance. They may at first sight seem purposefully fabricated, but a geologist who knows how they came to be there can usually explain their interesting shapes and properties. Suppose further, however, that the marks on this stone are found to resemble the characters of an ancient alphabet. This, too, does not prove that they were purposefully inscribed, for natural forces can leave such marks as these on stones, and over the course of millions of years it is entirely possible that this should occasionally happen. There are places where one can, at will, pick up stones that are almost perfect rectangles and look exactly as though they were hewn by stonecutters, though in fact they resulted from glaciation. But now suppose that these marks are recognized by a scholar having a knowledge of that alphabet, and that with considerable uncertainty due to the obscurity of some of the marks and the obliteration of others, he renders a translation of them as follows: HERE KIMON FELL LEADING A BAND OF ATHENIANS AGAINST THE FORCES OF XERXES. Now one can, to be sure, still maintain that the marks are accidental, that they are only scratches left by volcanic activity, and that it is only a singular coincidence that they resemble, more or less, some intelligible message. Nature sometimes produces effects hardly less interesting and arresting than this. The point to make again, however, is this: if anyone having a knowledge of this stone concludes, solely on the basis of it, that there was someone named Kimon who died in battle near where this stone was found, then he cannot, rationally, suppose that the marks on the stone are the result of the chance or purposeless operations of the forces of nature. He must, on the contrary, assume that they were inscribed there by someone whose purpose was to record an historical fact. If the marks had a purposeless origin, as from volcanic activity or whatnot, then they cannot reveal any fact whatever except, perhaps, certain facts about themselves or their origin. It would, accordingly, be irrational for anyone to suppose *both* that what is seemingly expressed by the marks is true, and *also* that they appeared as the result of nonpurposeful forces, provided the marks are his *sole* evidence for believing that what they seem to say is true.

Sensation and evidence   Our own organs of sense, to say nothing of our brains and nervous systems, are things of the most amazing and bewildering complexity and delicacy. No matter how far and minutely psychologists and physiologists press their studies of these organs, they seem hardly any closer to a real understanding of them, and how they enable us to *perceive* the world around us. At best they discover only how they convey stimuli and impress physical changes upon the brain. Theories of perception, drawing upon all the scientific and physiological knowledge accumulated to date, are hardly less crude than the speculations of the Greeks.

Some of these organs, moreover, strikingly resemble things purposefully designed and fabricated by men, though they greatly exceed in their delicacy and versatility anything men have invented. The parts and structure of the eye, for example, closely resemble those of a camera. Yet the comparison of these, however striking, is superficial, for the eye does not take pictures. Unlike a camera, it somehow enables its possessor to perceive and thereby to understand. Things like this can be more or less imitated by men, but they are usually crude and makeshift in comparison. It is sometimes almost irresistible, when considering such a thing as the eye, to suppose that, however it may have originated, it is constructed in that manner *in order* to enable its possessor to see. Many persons quite naturally think in these terms, without at all realizing the implications of such purposeful or teleological conceptions.

It must be noted, however, that just as it is possible for a collection of stones to present a novel and interesting arrangement on the side of a hill, and for marks to appear on a stone in a manner closely resembling some human artifact, and for these things still to be the accidental results of natural, nonpurposeful forces, so also it is possible for such things as our own organs of sense to be the accidental and unintended results, over ages of time, of perfectly impersonal, nonpurposeful forces. In fact, ever so many biologists believe that this is precisely what has happened, that our organs of sense are in no real sense purposeful things, but only appear so because of our failure to consider how they might have arisen through the normal workings of nature. It is supposed, for example, that if we apply the conceptions of chance mutations and variations, natural selection, and so on, then we can see how it is at least possible—perhaps even almost inevitable—that things of this sort should finally emerge, without any purpose behind them at all.

It would be astonishing indeed if a quantity of stones were hurled into the air and fell to earth in a pattern spelling out some intelligible message. Any man would feel, quite irresistibly, that it had been somehow *arranged* that they should fall that way. It would be less astonishing, however, if those stones were thrown a million times, and sooner or later fell to earth in such a pattern. Our astonishment would be still less if we found some perfectly natural, nonpurposeful explanation why they might sooner or later fall in that manner and, having so fallen, be thus preserved. If, for instance, we found that the stones were of slightly different weights, sizes and shapes, that these influenced how they were thrown and how they rolled upon landing, that these slight differences tended to favor the likelihood that certain ones would come to rest in the striking manner in which they do come to rest, and that certain obstructions on the ground would tend to preserve them in this arrangement, and so on, then we might find it entirely plausible how they might fall as they do without the intervention of any purposeful being at all. If our explanation were of this kind, however, then, as noted before, their arrangement would constitute no evidence whatever for anything not causally connected with themselves.

The mere complexity, refinement and seemingly purposeful arrangement of our sense organs do not, accordingly, constitute any conclusive reason for supposing that they are the outcome of any purposeful activity. A natural, nonpurposeful explanation of them is possible, and has been attempted—successfully, in the opinion of many.

The important point, however, and one that is rarely considered is that we do not simply *marvel* at these structures, and wonder how they came to be that way. We do not simply view them as amazing and striking things, and speculate upon their origins. We, in fact, whether justifiably or not, *rely* on them for the discovery of things that we suppose to be true and which we suppose to exist quite independently of those organs themselves. We suppose, without even thinking about it, that they reveal to us things that have nothing to do with themselves, their structures, or their origins. Just as we supposed that the stones on the hill told us that we were entering Wales—a fact having nothing to do with the stones themselves—so also we suppose that our senses in some manner "tell us" what is true, at least sometimes. The stones on the hill could, to be sure, have been an accident, in which case we cannot suppose that they really tell us anything at all. So also, our senses and all our faculties could be accidental in their origins, and in that case they do not really tell us anything either. But the fact remains, that we do trust them, without the slightest reflection on the matter. Our seeing something is often thought to be, quite by itself, a good reason for believing that the thing exists, and it would be absurd to suggest that we *infer* this from the structure of our eyes or speculations upon their evolutionary origins. And so it is with our other faculties. Our remembering something is often considered to be, quite by itself, a good reason for believing that the thing remembered did happen. Our hearing a sound is often considered, quite by itself, a good reason for believing that a sound exists; and so on.

We are not here suggesting that our senses are infallible, nor even, that we ought to rely upon their testimony. The point is that we do rely upon them. We do not believe merely that our senses are remarkably interesting things. We do not believe merely that they produce interesting effects within us, nor merely that they produce beliefs in us. We assume, rightly or wrongly, that they are *trustworthy* guides with respect to what is true, and what exists independently of our senses and their origins; and we still assume this, even when they are our only guides.

We saw that it would be irrational for anyone to say *both* that the marks he found on a stone had a natural, nonpurposeful origin and *also* that they reveal some truth with respect to something other than themselves, something that is not merely inferred from them. One cannot rationally believe both of these things. So also, it is now suggested, it would be irrational for one to say *both* that his sensory and cognitive faculties had a natural, nonpurposeful origin and *also* that they reveal some truth with respect to something other than themselves, something that is not merely inferred from them. *If their origin can be entirely accounted for in terms of chance variations, natural selection, and so on,* without supposing that they somehow embody and express the purposes of some creative being, then the most we can say of them is that they exist, that they are complex and wondrous in their construction, and are perhaps in other respects interesting and remarkable. We cannot say that they are, entirely by themselves, reliable guides to any truth whatever, save only what can be inferred from their own structure and arrangement. If, on the other hand, we do assume that they are guides to some truths having nothing to do with themselves, then it is difficult to see how we can, consistently with that supposition, believe them to have arisen by accident, or by the ordinary workings of purposeless forces, even over ages of time.

At this point persons who have a deep suspicion of all such arguments as this, and particularly persons who are hostile to any of the claims of religion, are likely to seize upon numberless objections of a sort that it would hardly occur to anyone to apply to our first two examples, involving the stones. Thus, it is apt to be said that our cognitive faculties are not so reliable as some would suppose, which is irrelevant; or that arguments from analogy prove nothing, which is also irrelevant, since none of the foregoing is an argument from analogy. Or it is claimed that we rely on our cognitive faculties only because we have found them reliable in the past, and thus have a sound inductive basis for our trust, which is absurd, if not question-begging. The reason I believe there is a world around me is, quite simply, that I see it, feel it, hear it, and am in fact perpetually in cognitive contact with it, or at least assume myself to be, without even considering the matter. To suggest that I *infer* its existence from the effects that it has within me, and that I find the inference justified on the ground that such inner effects have, in the past, been accompanied by external causes, is not only a ridiculous caricature, but begs the question of how, without relying upon my faculties, I could ever confirm such an idea in the first place. Again, it is sometimes said that the capacity to grasp truths has a decided value to the survival of an organism, and that our cognitive faculties have evolved, quite naturally, through the operation of this principle. This appears farfetched, however, even if for no other reason than that man's capacity to understand what is true, through reliance upon his senses and cognitive faculties, far exceeds what is needed for survival. One might as well say that the sign on the hill welcoming tourists to Wales originated over the course of ages purely by accident, and has been preserved by the utility it was then found to possess. This is of course possible, but also immensely implausible.

The significance It would be extravagant indeed to suppose that these reflections
of these amount to any sort of confirmation of religion, or even, that they
arguments have much to do with religion. They are purely metaphysical and
philosophical considerations having implications of only a purely
speculative kind. Even if they are utterly probative, which is of course
controversial, it can still be pointed out, correctly, that they are consistent with ever so many views which are radically inconsistent with
religion. They imply almost nothing with respect to any divine attributes, such as benevolence, and one could insist with some justification
that even the word God, which is supposed to be the proper name of a
personal being and not just a label to be attached to metaphysically
inferred things, is out of place in them.

No more is claimed for these arguments, however, than that they
are good arguments, and that they seem to yield the conclusions derived
from them. If they are defective, the defects are not gross or obvious.
The reader may suit himself whether they yield those conclusions, and
if so, what their human significance might be.

For
further
reading

Chapter 1 Persons and Bodies

McTaggart, J. M. E., "Personality," *Philosophical Studies*. London: Edward Arnold & Co., 1934.

Plato, *Phaedo, The Dialogues of Plato*, tr. B. Jowett. New York: Random House, 1937.

Ryle, Gilbert, *The Concept of Mind*. London: Hutchinson's University Library, 1949.

St. Thomas Aquinas, "Man: His Powers; His Knowledge," *Introduction to St. Thomas Aquinas*, ed. Anton C. Pegis. New York: Modern Library, Inc., 1948.

Wisdom, John, *Problems of Mind and Matter*, chapters 1-3. New York: Cambridge University Press, 1934.

Chapter 2 Interactionism

Descartes, R., *Passions of the Soul*, Part I, *Meditations*, particularly 1, 2, and 6, in *Descartes: Selections*, ed. R. M. Eaton. New York: Charles Scribner's Sons, 1927.

Ducasse, C. J., *Nature, Mind and Death*, particularly chapters 12, 14, 17, and 18. La Salle, Ill.: The Open Court Publishing Company, 1951.

Wisdom, John, *Problems of Mind and Matter*, chapters 4-7. New York: Cambridge University Press, 1934.

Chapter 3 The Mind as a Function of the Body

Hobbes, Thomas, *The Metaphysical System of Hobbes*, selected by Mary Whiton Calkins. La Salle, Ill.: The Open Court Publishing Company, 1948.

James, William, "The Automaton Theory," *The Principles of Psychology.* New York: Holt, Rinehart & Winston, Inc., 1890.

Whiteley, C. H., *An Introduction to Metaphysics,* chapters 1-5. London: Methuen & Co., Ltd., 1950.

Chapter 4 Freedom and Determinism

Ayer, A. J., "Freedom and Necessity," *Philosophical Essays.* London: Macmillan & Company, Ltd., 1954.

Broad, C. D., "Determinism, Indeterminism and Libertarianism," *Ethics and the History of Philosophy.* London: Routledge and Kegan Paul, Ltd., 1952.

Campbell, C. A., "Has the Self 'Free Will?' " *Selfhood and Godhood.* London: George Allen & Unwin, Ltd., 1957.

Fichte, J. G., "Doubt," *The Vocation of Man.* New York: Liberal Arts Press, Inc., 1956.

Hook, Sidney, ed. *Determinism and Freedom in the Age of Modern Science.* New York: New York University Press, 1958.

Hume, David, "Of Liberty and Necessity," *An Enquiry Concerning Human Understanding.* New York: Liberal Arts Press, Inc., 1955.

James, William, "The Dilemma of Determinism," *The Will to Believe and Other Essays.* New York: Longmans, Green & Co., Inc., 1927.

Melden, A. I., *Free Action.* London: Routledge and Kegan Paul, Ltd., 1961.

Ryle, Gilbert, "The Will," *The Concept of Mind.* London: Hutchinson's University Library, 1949.

Chapter 5 Fate

Aristotle, "De Interpretatione," *The Basic Works of Aristotle,* ed. Richard McKeon. New York: Random House, 1941.

Boethius, *The Consolation of Philosophy,* Book V, tr. W. V. Cooper. New York: Modern Library, Inc., 1943.

Cicero, *De Fato,* tr. H. Rackham. Cambridge: Loeb Classical Library, Harvard University Press, 1960.

Hartshorne, Charles, *Man's Vision of God,* chapter 3. Chicago: Willett, Clark & Co., 1941.

Ryle, Gilbert, "It Was to Be," *Dilemmas.* New York: Cambridge University Press, 1954.

Chapter 6 Time and Becoming

McTaggart, J. M. E., "The Unreality of Time," *Philosophical Studies.* London: Edward Arnold & Co., 1934.

Moore, G. E., "Is Time Unreal?" *Some Main Problems of Philosophy.* London: George Allen & Unwin, Ltd., 1953.

St. Augustine, *Confessions,* Book XI. London: Everyman's Library, J. M. Dent & Sons, Ltd., 1949.

Chapter 7 God

Gilson, E., *The Christian Philosophy of St. Thomas Aquinas*, Part I. London: Victor Gollancz, Ltd., 1957.

Hawkins, D. J. B., *The Essentials of Theism*. London: Sheed and Ward, Ltd., 1949.

Hume, David, *Dialogues Concerning Natural Religion,* ed. Norman Kemp Smith. Oxford: The Clarendon Press, 1935.

Leibniz, G. W., "On the Ultimate Origination of Things," *The Monadology and Other Philosophical Writings*, ed. Robert Latta. London: Oxford University Press, 1948.

Mascall, E. L., *He Who Is*. London: Longmans, Green & Co., Inc., 1954.

St. Thomas Aquinas, "God," *Introduction to St. Thomas Aquinas*, ed. Anton C. Pegis. New York: Modern Library, Inc., 1948.

Taylor, A. E., *Does God Exist?* London: Macmillan & Co., Ltd., 1948.

Whiteley, C. H., *An Introduction to Metaphysics*, chapters 9-10. London: Methuen & Co., Ltd., 1950.

INDEX

Daryl Smith